Learning
the essential
Sequence
Dances

D1321811

First published 1997

by

T. A. Whitworth,
42 Newbold Back Lane, Chesterfield,
Derbyshire, S40 4HQ.

ISBN 0-9501927-7-5

British Library Cataloguing in Publication Data:

Whitworth, Thomas Alan

Learning the Essential Sequence Dances

I. Title   II. Titanius

793.33

ISBN 0-9501927-7-5

Printed in Great Britain by:

Hillman Printers (Frome) Limited,
Frome, Somerset, BA11 4RW.

FOREWORD
by
DEREK ARNOLD

Welcome to the world of sequence dancing! —you have just taken the first steps to making sure that you enjoy the rest of your life - and live it to the full.

Sequence dancing is not only a way of meeting other people of like mind, and that is enjoyable in itself, it is the best way I know of ensuring that you enjoy a much richer and, indeed, a longer life. Research has shown that those who have taken up sequence dancing, even late in life, ensure through continually learning and then dancing new sequences that their memory functions and their physical well-being are enhanced, so much so that those taking up our dancing around the age of 55 to 65 can look forward to many extra years of happiness.

Many people took lessons when they were younger, and possibly practised their dancing in one of the many dance halls up and down the country. Most would learn modern ballroom dancing, a free-style in which the couples choose their own order of steps. Modern sequence, although based loosely upon modern ballroom dancing, is different in that all the dancers proceed anti-clockwise around the room doing the same steps as each other - each dance has a different name like Mayfair Quickstep or Sindy Swing. The steps for any of these dances are written down as a 'script' or choreograph and are described in such a way that qualified teachers who may never have seen the dance before can not only dance it straightaway - but teach it too.

As a person much concerned with sequence dancing and one of the main suppliers of scripts, I have always thought that there was a great need for another book in this area. What I had in mind was a collection of scripts of the most common sequence dances used for teaching purposes with detailed explanations of the terms used and notes on how to perform the dances. This would provide the newcomer with material to study outside the dancing sessions and speed up the learning process.

With this in mind I approached the author, Alan Whitworth, to see if he could put my ideas into print. I have known Alan for several years and have thought sufficiently well of his previous books to award him the Certificate of Merit for services to sequence dancing. I can recommend the final result - it is a book that should be on the shelves of all sequence dancers.

The Front Cover

The cover picture is of **George and Jill Stidwell** of Axbridge, Somerset; it is based on a photograph taken by **Pete Brownett** of Weston-super-Mare.

George and Jill are full-time professional dance teachers. In the winter season they work overseas for a large holiday company; in the summer they host dance holidays in the UK and run sequence dances in the Axbridge area.

The front and back covers and the frontispiece have been designed by **Dave Charlesworth** - one of Derbyshire's leading artists.

THE AUTHORS

Thomas Alan Whitworth has written the first two parts of the book. Section I deals with learning methods and explains the technical terms used in dance scripts. Section II contains the scripts of a variety of popular sequence dances with explanatory notes on their performance.

Alan Whitworth has published several books on sequence dancing - these are listed on the inside back cover. He sells and distributes these from his home address.

Titanius is the pen-name of the writer of Section III which takes a look at the lighter side of sequence dancing. The material consists mainly of articles written for 'The Ballroom Dancing Times', suitably amended and extended for this publication. The cartoons in this section and the illustrations throughout the book are the work of ***Les Barton***.

ACKNOWLEDGEMENTS

To ***Susan Baker*** for type-setting an awkward manuscript and advising on the layout.

To ***John Fay*** of Yeovil for providing many ideas for the book and being a source of advice and encouragement.

To ***Derek Arnold*** for being the instigator of the volume and for allowing free access to his several copyright collections of scripts. Derek is editor of the magazine 'Sequence Dancing World' and Director of North Star Publishers - suppliers of modern dance scripts and script collections.

AUTHOR'S NOTES

This volume is a source book for both sequence dancing teachers and beginners. For teachers it provides scripts of many of the sequence dances used for teaching purposes with some background material; for learners it will provide something to study away from the dancing sessions.

In general the dances in each chapter are arranged in order of increasing difficulty. To provide a varied programme the teacher will need to select dances from different parts of the book rather than moving through page by page. Dances notably easier than the rest include the Sweetheart Waltz, Harry Lime and Melody Foxtrots, Yearning Saunter, Lingering Blues, Lilac O/T Waltz, Eva Three Step and Rock Barn Dance.

Dance scripts not given in full in the text are to be found in two volumes available from North Star Publishers, P.O. Box 20, Otley, West Yorkshire, LS21 2SA:-

(a)   '66 Popular Modern Sequence Dances'
(b)   '66 Old-Time Dances'

The author wishes to express his gratitude to the many dancers who have (consciously or unconsciously!) helped him in his work. In particular he wishes to pay tribute to the dance leaders who gave unsparingly of their time and expertise to provide enjoyment for the many.

With love to my wife, Margaret, and family.

A.M.D.G.

T. A. Whitworth   **December 1997**

CONTENTS

SECTION I

LEARNING FROM DANCE SCRIPTS

SECTION II

SCRIPTS OF POPULAR SEQUENCE DANCES

SECTION III

THE LIGHTER SIDE OF SEQUENCE DANCING

DANCES WITH FULL SCRIPTS

DANCES WITH ABBREVIATED SCRIPTS

SECTION I

LEARNING FROM

DANCE SCRIPTS

All sequence dances can be described by dance scripts which state how the dances should be performed. Like knitting patterns these scripts use abbreviations and technical terms which are explained in this section.

After some introductory material the basic principles of script reading are set out in some detail to prepare the reader to make full use of the dance descriptions of Section II.

CHAPTER 1

THE NATURE OF SEQUENCE DANCING

Ballroom and Sequence Dancing

Nearly everyone has attended a social dance of some kind - a dance to raise funds, to celebrate some happy event or a dance in a hotel or holiday camp. The programmes for these events usually consist of a mixture of non-sequence and sequence dances.

Non-sequence dances are sometimes called go-as-you-please dances since the dancers choose their own order of steps and do their own thing. Ballroom dances like the waltz, quickstep, slow foxtrot and tango fall into this class. Other examples are the Latin-American dances (rumba, cha cha cha, samba, etc.) and the free-style dances (disco, rock and roll, twist, jive, etc.). These dances cater for a wide range of dancing ability from the absolute beginner to the trained dancer. They are somewhat informal - the dancers join in and finish dancing as the mood takes them.

Sequence dances in contrast have a pre-arranged order of steps which all perform together - something like formation dancing. The sequence can be written down in a dance script. Examples are old-time sequences (Veleta, St. Bernard Waltz), more modern 16-bar sequences (Mayfair Quickstep, Sindy Swing), fun dances (Hokey Cokey, Birdie Dance) and line dances (Slosh, American line dances). Simple dances of this type are readily learned since the sequences are repeated several times; they add welcome variety to a dancing programme.

3

SEQUENCE DANCING: THE INTENTION

WHEN THE MUSIC MISSES A BEAT!

Modern Sequence Dancing

One form of sequence dancing has become so popular that it has taken over the name. If you hear of someone going sequence dancing or taking a sequence dancing holiday it is generally understood that they will be performing 16-bar sequences in the style of the Balmoral Blues or Tango Serida - there are thousands of sequence dances arranged in this format. They are all partner dances for a man and a lady (or two ladies). The couples move round the ballroom in a more-or-less anti-clockwise direction, usually in ballroom or some other hold.

In sessions wholly devoted to sequence dancing it is usual to have a dance leader who announces each dance and then leads it off with his partner. After 1 or 2 sequences the majority join in - it is not a spectator sport! A normal programme will be some 15-20 different dances in a 2-3 hour session with a short interval for refreshments.

Dance Programmes

The dance leader, sometimes called the Master of Ceremonies or MC, usually chooses his list of dances and selects the music beforehand - experience will have given him some idea of the wishes of his clients. He has to allow a certain degree of flexibility to adapt to unforeseen circumstances - request dances, errors in leading off, birthday celebrations, etc. Most leaders will introduce new dances from time to time noting carefully the reactions of the group - if there is too much change the dancers may move elsewhere! In general dancers turning out several nights per week like some degree of variety and challenge whereas those who dance less often prefer a more static programme.

Before attending any sequence dancing session it is a wise precaution to find out something about the nature of the dances to be performed if one wishes to be a dancer rather than a spectator. This is particularly important for beginners who have a smaller repertoire and take longer to master unfamiliar dances. Some of the main types of dancing session are described below.

(a)   Social (Club) Dances

Programmes do not vary much from week to week and dancers attending regularly soon master the sequences by watching others. Most dances are from the 1950-1975 period with some older favourites such as the Square Tango and Lingering Blues. Dancing clubs meeting in schools and church halls have a leader and recorded music; in licensed premises an organist usually announces and plays the music for the sequences. These clubs play a useful role in preserving the best of the older dances. Newcomers to sequence dancing often attend these sessions to practise their skills without feeling under too much pressure.

(b)   Modern Sequence Dancing Sessions

New official sequence dances are winners of first prizes in inventive dance competitions recognised by the Official Board. There are usually 45 dances each year divided equally between the old-time, modern and Latin-American styles. The programmes for modern sequence dancing sessions consist mainly of the latest of these dances along with some favourites from earlier years. These are sessions for the enthusiasts - dancing for them is a way of life rather than a casual form of entertainment. Some dancers attend 4-7 evenings per week for years on end to keep up-to-date as the programmes change month by month; more experienced dancers may get by with 2 or 3 sessions each week. Some sequence dancing sessions are intermediate in standard and only some of the new dances are taught - old-time waltzes, gavottes, two-steps, jives and sambas are often omitted.

(c)   Old-Time Dancing Sessions

Old-time dancing is still popular today but less so than the modern style. The programmes contain mainly dances arranged before 1958 with some square dances for 4 couples like the Lancers. Later dances like the Balmoral Blues (1971) and Sindy Swing (1984) are often included but care is taken to avoid being 'too modern'. Although there is a wide repertoire of old-time dances the programmes do not vary greatly over time compared with modern sequence dancing sessions - it is not too difficult for anyone to pick up the threads after an absence due to holidays or illness. Like modern sequence dancing sessions, few couples sit out and the refreshments form a welcome break to the dancing.

(d)   Tea Dances - Mixed Sessions

Some 'tea' dances and holiday sessions where the clientele changes from week to week have programmes which try to satisfy the needs of both ballroom and sequence dancers. They are sometimes called 50-50 dances but the proportions may vary widely from almost all sequence (North of England) to nearly all ballroom and go-as-you-please dances (South East).

Mixed sessions of this type are very useful for aspiring sequence dancers to help them acquire the basic skills, particularly if the ballroom floor is large enough to give them room to make the occasional mistake without becoming a hazard to other dancers.

Classification of Sequence Dances

Since 1975 all new 'official' sequence dances have to be winners at inventive dance competitions recognised by the Official Board (from 1996 called the British Dance Council). Dance leaders are discouraged from including 'unofficial' dances in their sessions. At the present time there are competitions sponsored by 15 bodies, each awarding prizes in the 3 sections below making 45 new official dances per year.

(a) **Old-Time (Classical) Section**
O/T Waltz, O/T Tango, Saunter, Swing, Blues, Gavotte, Two Step, Mazurka, Schottische, Glide, Sway, etc.

(b) **Modern Section**
Mod. Waltz, Mod. Tango, Quickstep, Slow Foxtrot, Viennese Waltz.

(c) **Latin-American Section**
Rumba, Cha Cha Cha, Samba, Jive, Paso Doble, Bossa Nova, etc.

Technique and composition of sequences for any particular dance such as an old-time and modern tango are also controlled by the Board - if a new arrangement diverges too much from standard practice it will not win an award and become a new 'official' sequence dance.

New Official Dances, 1990-1995

Tango	44	Swings	11
Rumba	39	Gavottes	9
Mod. Waltz	35	Blues	7
Cha Cha Cha	28	Samba	6
Saunter	27	O/T Waltz	5
Foxtrot	22	Two Step	2
Quickstep	18	Bossa Nova	2
Jives	15	*Total*	*270*

1996 has seen the appearance of a paso doble, a mambo, a mazurka and a swing with line dance elements. There is no doubt that the new dances give life and interest to the sequence dancing movement and prevent stagnation. Attendances at modern sequence dancing sessions rise when the new dances appear, and fall off when there are no competitions towards the end of the year.

Origins of Sequence Dancing

Old-time sequence dances for couples appeared in the 1850s becoming really popular from 1900 to 1924. Most sequences had old-time waltz elements and there were dances with hopping steps like the schottische, polka and mazurka. Technique derived from ballet was used with the feet at an angle and steps being taken more on the toes. From 1910 onwards dances with a more modern walking style like the tango, saunter and blues were added to the repertoire. There was a great revival in old-time dancing after the war but the more modern style began to take over. From 1960 to 1965 the ballroom associations began to show more interest in modern sequence dancing and by 1975 it was largely under their control. A fuller account of these matters can be found in the author's 'A History of Modern Sequence Dancing and Script List' *(1995)*.

CHAPTER 2

ASPECTS OF LEARNING

The Learning Process

Performing a sequence dance entails remembering the sequence and carrying out the steps in such a way as not to cause undue hindrance to others. Mind and body must work in harmony. In the early stages the mind is very active - later on the body takes over and the movements become more automatic. Car driving is very similar - in the beginning the learner thinks about gear lever and pedals but before long he drops into the right gear without conscious thought.

Practice is the secret of success and the learner's progress will be slow if the dancing (or driving) is confined to a weekly teaching session. For the aspiring sequence dancer this is a 'Catch 22' situation - to learn the skills practice is needed but effective practice requires a degree of competence. To attend even the simplest full-time sequence dancing session requires a basic repertoire of some 10-15 of the dances likely to appear on the programme if the partners are to be performers rather than spectators. They may well be among dancers who have met together for years and know their dances inside out - joining in with them is like learning to drive a car in a full stream of traffic without the instructor!

One objective of this book is to speed up the learning process in this difficult period by providing material to study outside the dancing sessions. To know something about the dancing figures and sequences will give learners more confidence and encourage them to persist. Partners may come away from a teaching session saying, "We've almost mastered that dance - let's try it out at home," only to find that they cannot remember the sequence exactly. It is one thing to dance in class to music surrounded by couples doing the steps more-or-less correctly - quite another to perform the dance as a solo couple in a restricted space! A copy of the dance script with explanatory notes will at least provide some degree of back-up here.

Learning by Watching Other Dancers

One of the secrets of successful sequence dancing is careful observation. Continued practice in this sharpens the mind - a benefit for the more mature! Just as leaving out a comma in a computer programme may cause a minor disaster, so omitting a chassé or a twinkle will leave the dancer standing on the foot he needs to move with - a common problem for learners!

The learning process is greatly assisted by watching other dancers - the dance leaders, others on the floor or performers on video. All sequence dancers (consciously or unconsciously) watch surrounding couples on the floor to avoid collisions, to check up their steps and alignments and sometimes out of mere curiosity!

Some dancers take no formal lessons of any kind and rely solely on watching couples moving round the floor. This approach is common among club dancers and those whose interest in sequence dancing is marginal. On the whole these dancers remember the sequences very well but their technique leaves something to be desired - saunters, tangos and slow foxtrots often tend to look much the same! Progress using this method tends to be slow and uncertain and the range of dances is restricted; faults in steps and technique can be readily picked up from others.

MAKING A START
One can follow other dancers ~

or a video tape ~

*Problems arise with both methods
once you start to turn!*

Learning from Videos

Several older works on sequence dancing have photographs taken at various stages in the sequences. These 'stills' have been largely superseded by video tapes which record the dancers in motion. Some excellent commercial videos have recently become available which include many of the dances described in this book.

Videos are very useful to beginners since the sequence dance can be seen as often as desired - both the order of steps and the manner of performance of the various dancing figures by experts can be studied at leisure.

Another approach is to persuade someone to take a video recording of your partner and yourself actually performing on the dance floor. You cannot usually see yourself dancing and your best friends will be loath to point out your deficiencies! It must be said that most dancers (even dance leaders) seem to be disappointed when they see the results - their comforting illusions are often shattered!

Group Teaching Sessions

The most popular method of learning (particularly for the more mature) is to attend group teaching sessions operated on a regular basis by a dance teacher. Here the most popular dances are 'stepped through' and then practised by the class as a whole. The repertoire is gradually extended with on-going discussion of theory and technique - during the dances the teacher will often call out the various dancing figures to remind the couples of what to do next. Many dance teachers operate practice sessions on different nights in addition and these are invaluable for beginners.

One disadvantage of this method is that some slow learners and inexperienced dancers may find it difficult to execute the figures straightaway - let alone remember them an hour later! Since others in the group will often pick up the steps immediately this can make the beginner feel inadequate, frustrated and disillusioned.

Group Learning — Dancing Figures

Studying with an Expert

Another alternative is to take private lessons from a teacher of dancing. This is more expensive but progress will be more rapid since errors and faults in technique can be corrected at an early stage. The teacher can see your difficulties at a glance and has the necessary authority and expertise to give you advice. Some slow learners may, however, feel uncomfortable when performing under the eagle eye of the instructor!

Ballroom dancers teach dancing figures and lay great emphasis on style of performance. If these figures are learnt correctly it is not too difficult to adapt to modern sequence. Teaching by a qualified teacher is really the only way to achieve a high standard of performance.

One can learn from a competent teacher.

Learning from Dance Scripts

Any sequence dance can be described by a dance script which sets out the order of steps and other relevant details - it is like the musical score for the musician. A modern dance script is a set of instructions which contains enough information for someone to perform the dance who might never have seen it demonstrated. Dance leaders often have to learn new dances from the script - not everyone can attend the inventive dance competitions and be taught by the winners.

One can learn from a script ~

What's this bota fogos?

Being able to read a dance script is more or less essential for dance leaders. It is a useful skill also for the ordinary dancer giving help in sorting out problems with particular steps and deepening the understanding of the dancing process. Scripts of some of the more popular dances appear in this volume with hints on performance and interpretation. Scripts of thousands of sequence dances are readily available from suppliers.

Learning from Dancing Figures

Describing a dance sequence on paper is not all that easy. The man's and lady's steps usually differ and alignments, amount of turn, timing, dance holds, etc. need to be specified. On average a 16-bar sequence for a waltz or slow foxtrot will contain about 48 steps, for a cha cha cha with 5 steps per bar this will rise to around 80. These are large numbers to deal with and it is convenient to group the steps into units called *dancing figures* (just as letters are made into words).

Dancing figures vary in size from the 1 step of the 'reverse pivot' in the quickstep to the 30 steps of the 'Turkish towel' in the cha cha cha.

One way of learning dancing figures is by the use of **foot diagrams**. 'Ballroom Dancing' by Alex Moore (A. and C. Black, reprinted 1992) has good foot diagrams for many dancing figures. Combining foot diagrams for man and lady has its advantages but makes the resulting pattern more complex.

LEARNING FROM FOOT DIAGRAMS

Dancing figures are the 'building bricks' for dances. In ballroom dancing each pair will use them to make a dancing pattern of their own; in sequence dancing the arranger will put together his figures (often from different dances) to make a pleasing 16-bar sequence which all will perform. Dancing figures are very useful in learning and remembering sequence dances. The dance leader will often call out the appropriate figures such as 'whisk', 'wing' and 'open telemark' to teach a new dance or refresh memories of an older dance. You will sometimes hear experienced dancers watching a new sequence and converting it into a string of dancing figures before they take the floor. A good knowledge of dancing figures is essential to the aspiring sequence dancer as this is the language by which information is passed between dancers - groupings of steps can be stored in the mind (and feet) for recall on a future occasion.

Approaches to Dance Teaching

There are two main methods of teaching sequence dancing, each with its own particular advantages and disadvantages.

Ballroom dancing teachers teach figures for each dance in turn - they consider that a dance such as the slow foxtrot has a certain walk and style and figures of its own. These figures are studied in detail with particular attention to technique and style of performance and pupils are encouraged to enter for the examinations of the various ballroom associations. Having mastered these figures it is then not too difficult to put them together, to dance a sequence slow foxtrot. They teach 'dancing' rather than sequence dances and the progression is from dancing figures to sequence dances. This approach is followed in the author's 'Modern Sequence Dancing For All' (1994) which has charts of many dancing figures but only two scripts. It differs from conventional ballroom manuals in that dancing figures are classified by foot movements rather than by style of dance - this was thought to be more appropriate for sequence dancing where a figure from one dance is used in other dances, thus the curved feather from the slow foxtrot is found also in waltzes and quicksteps.

The alternative approach is to teach sequence dances rather than dancing figures. The figures will then emerge naturally - in time the dancers will associate the names with the groupings of steps they perform week after week. Mature entrants to sequence dancing often prefer this approach as they wish to join others on the floor at sequence dancing sessions at an early stage rather than take the longer path of mastering the figures for each dance in turn. This method of moving from sequence dances to dancing figures is used in the sections which follow - there are many descriptions of dances but few charts of dancing figures. Surprisingly the overlap between the two books is relatively small - they can be regarded as two complementary approaches to the learning process for sequence dancers.

Tips for Learning Sequence Dances

(a) Dance as often as you can.

(b) Try and translate the movements into the appropriate dancing figures and study them from a book when you get home.

(c) Relate the dancing figures to one another to help memory and recall - look for similarities between the various dances.

(d) Take every opportunity to watch dancers carefully - you can learn also from people who make mistakes!

CHAPTER 3

BASIC THEORY

Introduction

Dance scripts are the main method of preserving and transmitting information relating to sequence dancing. At first sight scripts seem rather forbidding to the reader as they contain many abbreviations and specialist terms. There are good reasons, however, for using this format - space is saved and the relevant information is grasped more readily once the language has been learnt. Thus *'RF bk DC agst LOD'* conveys the meaning far more effectively than 'right foot back diagonal to centre against the line of dance' - the message can be lost in the mass of words.

This chapter is really a reference section for the remainder of the book - it might well be skipped through in a preliminary reading since some of the ideas are not easily grasped without some experience of dancing. It might be better for a beginner to attempt one of the dances listed (in class or elsewhere), study the script and refer back to this chapter if necessary.

Some Useful Abbreviations

LOD	line of dance	agst LOD	against line of dance
W	wall	DW	diagonal to wall
C	centre	DC	diagonal to centre
LF	left foot	RF	right foot
fwd	forward	bk	backward
fcg	facing	bkg	backing
ptg	pointing	tng	turning
comm	commencing	twd	towards

A more comprehensive list of abbreviations is to be found at the end of this chapter on page 36.

Line of Dance (LOD)

Sequence dances are progressive round dances in which couples circulate round the floor in a general anticlockwise direction. Foot positions and directions of motion in the ballroom are all related to the line of dance (LOD). In a circular ballroom, dancers moving down the line of dance trace out an anticlockwise circular path. Movement in the opposite clockwise direction is said to be against the line of dance (agst LOD).

Oval Ballroom

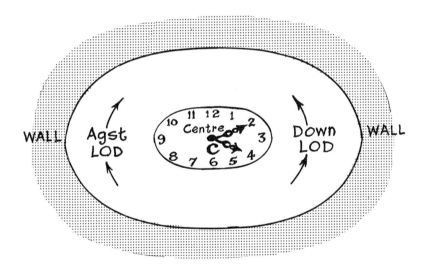

The edge of the floor is known as the **wall (W)** - a dancer facing the wall has his back to the **centre (C)**.

Using script writers' language:-

'Fcg W' (feet facing wall) is the same orientation as 'bkg C' (heels directed to centre).
'Fcg dn LOD' is the same as 'bkg agst LOD' (see later).

Rectangular Ballroom

In rectangular ballrooms the line of dance changes abruptly through a right angle at each corner to form a new line of dance. Moving down both the original and the new line of dance the dancer has the wall to the right and the centre to the left. Notice that the centre is not now the geometric centre of the room but a rectangular area.

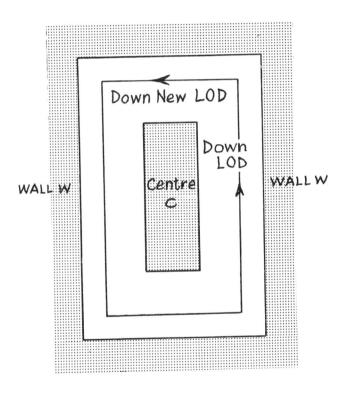

The turns at the corners of the room pose problems for dancers. Ballroom dancers choose a suitable figure such as a **natural** turn to the right to change direction. The sequence dancer, however, cannot choose - if a **reverse** turn (to the left) comes up at a corner he will find that 90° has been added to his normal amount of turn!

Positions in the Ballroom (The Compass Diagram)

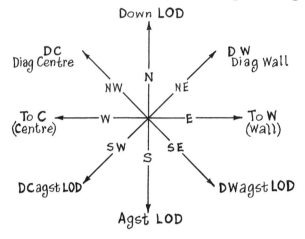

Positions of the feet are specified in relation to 'down LOD' just as north is used as the reference point on a map. A movement from one principal direction to the next involves a turn of ⅛, thus from DW to W (NE to E) is a clockwise turn of ⅛ (or an anticlockwise turn of ⅞).

These days the term *alignment* is used to indicate the orientation of the foot at the end of a step. The angle of rotation in a turn can be determined from the initial and final alignments - thus a change from 'down LOD' to DW is a clockwise turn of ⅛; from W to C is a rotation of ½ and so on.

Sometimes the directions on the diagram are used to specify movement rather than position - these are called 'directional terms'. *Direction* in this special sense is defined as the movement of the foot (or body) in relation to the ballroom. In the chassé from promenade position in the waltz the feet and body face DW (the alignment) but the body moves along the LOD (the directional term). Directional terms are often used in scripts of modern tangos.

Angles of Turn

A **natural** turn is a turn to the right; a **reverse** turn is a turn to the left.

Complete turn (1) 360°
The result of a complete turn is that the dancers face their original direction.

Half turn (½) 180°
A dancer taking a half turn will face in the opposite direction, e.g. from facing LOD to backing LOD.

Three-eighths turn (⅜) 135°
In a modern waltz natural turn the man turns through an angle of ¼ between steps 1 and 2 and a further ⅛ between steps 2 and 3 making ⅜ in all. The change in alignment is often from facing DW to backing LOD - clockwise through 3 compass positions.

Quarter turn (¼) 90°
Quarter turns are common in sequence dances although they are often not described as such. They sometimes result from underturning a figure with a ⅜ turn. Progressive chassés and zig-zags often involve quarter turns.

One-eighth turn (⅛) 45°
This is often described as a slight turn in the script or as turning a little more to left or right. These turns are often used to make a minor adjustment to get the dancers properly in line for the figure which is to follow.

Alignments

The alignment of a foot gives its position in relation to the room, i.e. its orientation with respect to the line of dance using the 'compass' positions like down LOD, DC or DW agst LOD. Alignments at the end of a step are the usual method of indicating the angle of turn in modern dances like the quickstep, slow foxtrot and waltz. When body and feet are in line there are two alternative ways of describing the alignment:-

(a) **Facing (fcg)** is the forward direction through the toe; it is used when the figure involves a forward movement, e.g. facing LOD when the next step is forward.

(b) **Backing (bkg)** is the backward direction through the heel. It is used when the general direction of movement is backward, e.g. bkg agst LOD before a backward step.

Pointing (ptg) is used when the feet and body are at an angle, e.g. the 5th step for the man (and the 2nd step for the lady) in the normal waltz turn. Here the body turns slightly less than the feet and body and feet are brought into line on the following step.

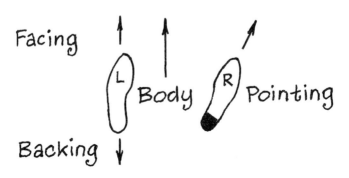

Alignments and Angles of Turn

Dancing turns are among the most complex of figures found in sequence dancing. Steps for man and lady are often different at different stages of the turn. These problems increase as the angle of turn gets larger - for turns of a quarter or less the lady's steps are usually just opposite to those of the man. Many modern scripts express the degree of rotation as a difference between the original and final alignments of the feet. Many dancers, however, feel more comfortable with an angle of turn and it is useful to be able to convert from one form to the other.

Angles between directions on the compass diagram are easily determined - there are 8 principal directions each at an angle of ⅛ to the next. Moving clockwise from down LOD (north) to DW (north east) is a turn of ⅛. Remember, however, that an anticlockwise turn of ⅞ will produce the same result! On the compass diagram the angles are measured relative to a fixed centre point - in many dancing turns there is progression down the line of dance (or some other direction) as well as rotation and this needs to be taken into account in working out the angle.

Determining angles of turn from alignments is made more difficult by the use of the terms 'facing' and 'backing' - this notation is very convenient for indicating the general flow of the dance but has its drawbacks. Many script readers (consciously or unconsciously) convert all the directions to facing before deducing the angle. These matters are more easily understood by using diagrams and considering actual examples. In the following section the reverse turn in the modern waltz is looked at in some detail.

The Waltz Reverse Turn

Groups of steps called *dancing figures* are used by ballroom dancers for teaching purposes. These are described in great detail in *charts* which set out clearly how the various steps have to be performed to gain the various awards. The waltz reverse turn is an example of a standard dancing figure. It has 6 steps with a total turn of ¾ to the left. Some information from a dancing chart of this figure is set out below.

| Steps | Reverse Turn (man's steps) | | |
	Foot Positions	Alignments	Amount of Turn
1	LF fwd	Fcg DC	Start to turn L
2	RF to side	Bkg DW	¼ between 1 and 2
3	LF closes to RF	Bkg LOD	⅛ between 2 and 3
4	RF back	Bkg LOD	Continue tng L
5	LF to side	Ptg DW	⅜ between 4 and 5
6	RF closes to LF	Fcg DW	Body completes turn

The lady does steps 4-6 while man does steps 1-3 (although the alignments differ) and vice versa.

In the table above *foot position* gives the relation of one foot to the other *at the end of the step*, e.g. on step 2 the LF swivels during the turn and the RF finishes to the side of the LF. In the same way the *alignment* gives the orientation (compass bearing) of the foot at the *end of the step*.

An alternative way of representing the data in the table is the foot diagram opposite. Angles of turn and step length are easily seen as well as foot positions and alignments at various stages of the turn. Unfortunately foot diagrams for many of the figures used in sequence dances are not readily available.

Angles and Alignments in the Reverse Turn

The steps are numbered as in the table on the preceding page; dotted lines in the foot diagram indicate that the foot has swivelled from its original position.

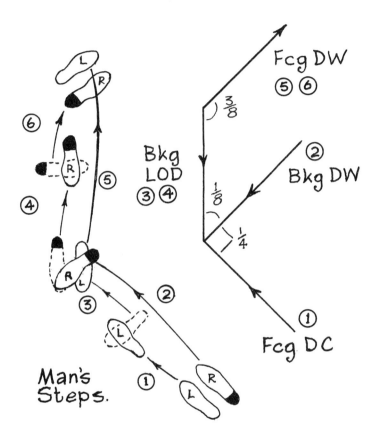

Man's Steps.

Steps	Angle	Alignments
1-2	¼	Fcg DC to Bkg DW
2-3	⅛	Bkg DW to Bkg LOD
4-5	⅜	Bkg LOD to Ptg DW
6	-	Body completes turn fcg DW

Further Notes on the Reverse Turn

Steps:-

1 *LF fwd DC starting to turn L*
   LF moves forward in a straight line diagonal to centre; body turns slightly L preparing for the turn.

2 *RF to side bkg DW (across the LOD)*
   As RF moves forward the LF swivels through ¼ to the L. At the end of the step the LF and RF are parallel at some distance apart. The heels of both feet are directed diagonally to the wall (bkg DW).

3 *LF closes to RF now bkg LOD*
   Man's body and feet now turn ⅛ L to face against the LOD - expressed as *'bkg LOD'* (heels directed down LOD) since the next step is backward.

4 *RF bk down LOD tng L*
   As the RF moves back the body turns slightly left.

5 *LF to side ptg DW (along the LOD)*
   LF to the side with the toe pointing diagonally to the wall. Pointing is used since feet and body are not in line on this step - body is facing the wall.

6 *RF closes to LF fcg DW*
   The man's body completes the turn and feet and body now face diagonally to wall; the lady is backing diagonal to wall.

Waltz time is 3 beats per bar and taking 1 step for each beat means that the complete turn will occupy 2 bars. This is really a mini-script - there are 14 bars more to come in the normal 16-bar sequence dance! Fortunately, after dancing for a while, 'reverse turn' conjures up all this information - feet and body perform the turn correctly without conscious effort.

Foot Positions

The foot position gives the spacial relationship of one foot to the other at the end of the step. Thus step 1 of the waltz reverse turn is *'LF fwd DC tng L'*. At the end of the step the foot position is LF forward of RF (the alignment is DC).

Some terms used in foot positions are:-

- Forward; Diagonally forward
- To side; To side and slightly forward; To side and slightly backward
- Backward; Diagonally backward
- Foot crosses in front or behind
- Promenade and fallaway positions

Promenade Position (PP) - Partners are in a V-shaped position with the man's right side near the lady's left side. **Fallaway Position** is achieved from PP by the partners stepping back with outside feet and turning outwards.

Promenade Position

Counter Promenade

Counter Promenade Position (CPP) - This is promenade position with positions interchanged - the man's L side is near the lady's R side.

Contrary Body Movement (CBM) - The opposite hip and shoulder are turned to the direction of the step being taken, e.g. as the left foot moves forward, so do the right hip and right shoulder. The momentum for turns in dances like the waltz and quickstep comes largely from the 'swing' of the opposite hip and shoulder; good examples are the spin and pivot turns. CBM is a body movement and is not mentioned in dance scripts.

Contrary Body Movement Position (CBMP) - The foot is placed on or across the line of the stationary foot (either in front or behind) without turning the body. It gives a similar appearance to CBM without the body movement. It is a foot placing and appears in scripts and dancing figures (see following pages). CBMP is used on every outside step, and step with partner outside, to maintain body contact; it is found in some other figures such as the change in direction in the foxtrot. In scripts CBMP is not always mentioned particularly if space is at a premium - it is assumed that the dancer will adopt this position when taking a step outside partner.

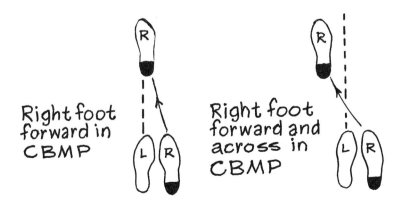

Right foot forward in CBMP

Right foot forward and across in CBMP

Shoulder leading - The same side of the body as the stepping foot moves forward (or backward) - it is the opposite of CBM. Unlike CBM it alters slightly the positions of the feet and is mentioned in scripts and charts of dancing figures. A shoulder-leading step will often follow a step in CBMP and vice versa - one reverses the effect of the other. Shoulder-leading has an opening-out movement which tends to reverse the locking effect of a step in CBMP.

Examples:-

(a) Feather Step; Slow Foxtrot (man's steps)

    1 RF fwd
    2 LF fwd, L shoulder leading preparing to step outside partner (OP)
    3 RF fwd in CBMP outside partner (OP)
    4 LF fwd partner in line (partner square)

Step 3 reverses the opening-out effect of step 2.

(b) Forward Walk; Modern Tango (man's steps)

    1 LF fwd in CBMP DW curving slightly left
    2 RF down LOD, shoulder leading

Locking effect of step 1 reversed by step 2.

Outside Partner (OP) - A forward step outside the partner instead of in line - usually taken to the right.

Partner Outside (PO) - This is the partner's step corresponding to OP. It is not usually mentioned in foot positions as it is the one who is moving forward who creates the position.

Across and Along the Line of Dance

These terms are sometimes found in older scripts. They give direction of movement and some indication of the foot position but not alignment. Imagine a straight line passing through the foot you are standing on and directed down the line of dance. If the moving foot finishes on this line this is expressed as **along the line of dance**, if the line is crossed by the foot this is **across the line of dance**.

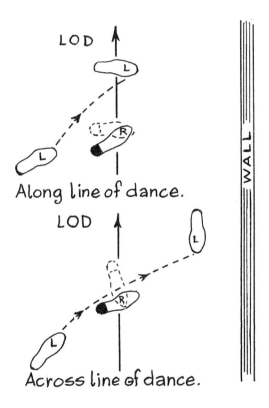

Moving across the line of dance occurs on the second step of most dancing turns involving a turn of ½ or more on the first 3 steps, e.g. man's step 2 of the waltz reverse turn is *'RF to side bkg DW'* or *'RF to side across LOD'*.

Directional Terms

Directional terms specify the direction of movement of the foot in relation to the room. If feet and body have the same alignment as the general direction of motion the direction of motion is clear from the foot position and alignment.

Suppose a man starts a dance facing DW and his first step is 'LF fwd DW'. At the end of the step the LF is forward of the RF (foot position). The LF is oriented DW (alignment). The direction of movement is 'LF fwd DW' - the foot is moving in front of the body in direction DW.

An extra directional term is needed for the man's first step in the chassé from promenade position in the modern waltz:-

RF fwd and across in PP and CBMP facing DW, moving along LOD

'RF fwd and across in PP and CBMP' is the **foot position**, 'facing DW' is the **alignment**, 'moving along LOD' is the **directional term**.

Feet and body are facing DW on all 4 steps but the direction of movement is along (down) LOD.

Separate directional terms are rarely found in the modern waltz, slow foxtrot and quickstep but are widely used in the modern tango and other dances. Dancing charts for the modern tango use the heading 'Direction or Alignment' instead of 'Alignment' since feet and body are often at an angle to the general direction of motion. The most common directional terms are 'along (down) LOD' and 'against LOD'. In a script it is not always easy to distinguish between alignment, foot position and the directional term but the meaning is usually clear.

Abbreviations

acr	across	mvg	moving
ag, agst	against	opp	opposite
bhd	behind	OP	outside partner
bk(g)	back (backing)	PO	partner outside
br(g)	bring(ing)	posn	position
cls(g)	close (closing)	prep(g)	prepare(ing)
comm(g)	commence(ing)	PP	promenade
cv(g)	curve (curving)		position
C	centre	prog	progressive
CBM	contrary body	prom	promenade
	movement	ptg	pointing
CBMP	contrary body	ptnr	partner
	movement	Q	quick
	position	R	right
CPP	counter	RF	right foot
	promenade	RH	right hand
	position	rev	reverse
diag	diagonal(ly)	rsd, rsg	raised, raising
dn	down	S	slow
DC	diagonal to	sdw	shadow
	centre	shldr	shoulder
DW	diagonal to	s-by-s	side-by-side
	wall	sltly	slightly
fcg	facing	sq	square
fwd	forward	ss	small step
ldg	leading	swiv(g)	swivel(ling)
L	left	trans	transfer
LF	left foot	twds	towards
LH	left hand	tn, tng	turn(ing)
LOD	line of dance	ww	without weight

CHAPTER 4

DANCE SCRIPTS

All scripts have headings which contain some or all of the following:-

- the name, arranger and date of the dance
- any prizes awarded in competitions
- the initial alignments of the partners
- the dance hold
- titles of suitable music
- time signature and suggested tempo

Starting Alignment

Starting facing in the right direction is a great help in performing a sequence dance or any dancing figure - it helps with turns and collisions with others are less likely. For dances starting in **ballroom hold** there are 3 main alignments:-

(a)   **Down LOD** (man facing, lady backing) - early modern waltzes, tangos, saunters.

(b)   **Diagonal to Centre (DC)** - dances starting with a reverse turn, reverse cross, walk and feather, etc.

(c)   **Diagonal to Wall (DW)** - dances in which a turn to the right is imminent: e.g. step, natural turn; closed change, spin turn.

In earlier times rotary turns through ½ were often used. In modern dances the smaller angle of ⅜ is preferred since it leads to a more elegant figure which is easier to perform. Starting facing DC or DW gives the extra ⅛ which helps the turn on its way.

Ballroom Hold

This is the standard hold for the modern waltz, quickstep and slow foxtrot. In the modern tango hold the lady is more to the right - the partners stand obliquely to the line of dance with the man's right hip and shoulder forward.

Other Holds

Side by Side Position

Double Hold ～

Two Shadow Holds

Music for Sequence Dancing

Some older scripts state the title of the music to be used or sometimes a choice of melodies. Sometimes music and dance may have the same name as in the Veleta or Maxina. Always using the same music for a particular dance brings back memories and helps with remembering and timing of the steps - it may, however, become boring if the dance is performed too frequently. The modern practice is to specify the time signature and the tempo of the dance and leave the choice of music to the dance leader.

Beats and Bars

Music for dancing has a background of **beats** which are accentuated by bass and percussion instruments. Beats are easily picked out in music for the samba and modern tango - it is easy to tap one's foot to the beat. In music for the slow foxtrot the beats are more difficult to discern.

The beats receive different amounts of stress - this is called the pulse of the music. The same pattern of stressed beats occurs regularly throughout and dance music can be split up into **bars** on this basis. Each bar has the same time length and contains the same number of beats. Thus in music for waltzes and minuets there are 3 beats in each bar with the first beat accentuated.

Most dances are performed to music with 4 beats in the bar, the normal stress being heavy on beat 1, weak on beat 2, medium on beat 3 and weak on beat 4. There are various musical devices for displacing and missing beats which are used to produce new and exciting dance rhythms. Sometimes the basic rhythm extends over more than one bar.

Time Signature

The time signature is a measure of bar length. Hence corresponding bar lengths are:-

- for 4/4 time 4 x ¼ notes (4 crochets)
- for 6/8 time 6 x ⅛ notes (6 quavers/3 crochets)

The upper figure usually gives the number of beats per bar:-

- 3 beats per bar for 3/4 (waltz time)
- 2 beats per bar for 2/4 (tango time)

Tempo

In sequence dancing the speed of the music is expressed in bars per minute (bpm). Thus the recommended tempo for the modern waltz is 30-32 bpm. (Note that in line dancing the tempo is often specified in **beats** per minute.)

The right tempo for a dance is most important - if too slow the music drags and it is difficult to maintain correct balance, if too fast the steps cannot be performed in comfort.

Playing Speeds (Tempi)

The recommended speeds for the various dances measured in bars per minute are set out in the following table:-

Section	Dance	Time signature	Tempo (bpm)	
Modern	Waltz	3/4	31	(29-31)
	Slow Foxtrot	4/4	30	(28-31)
	Quickstep	4/4	50	(45-50)
	Tango	2/4	33	(30-34)
	(Viennese Waltz)	3/4	60	(56-64)
(Feet at an angle)	O/T Waltz	3/4	42	(40-44)
	Gavotte	4/4	24	(23-25)
	Two Step	6/8	48	(44-56)
Old-Time ------	Mazurka	3/4	42	(42-46)
	Glide	4/4	24	(23-25)
	Saunter	4/4	28	(27-29)
	Blues	4/4	30	(29-31)
(Feet parallel)	Swing	4/4	48	(45-50)
	Old-Time Tango	2/4	32	(30-33)
Latin-American	Rumba	4/4 or 2/4	28	(26-32)
	Cha Cha Cha	4/4 or 2/4	30	(31-33)
	Samba	2/4 or 4/4	50	(48-54)
	Jive	4/4	44	(35-46)
	Paso Doble	2/4 or 6/8	62	(58-62)

For examination purposes each type of sequence dance has a fixed tempo, e.g. 50 bpm for the quickstep. In ordinary sequence dancing a range of speeds is used indicated by the figures in brackets - (45-50) bpm for the quickstep. Slower playing speeds are used for learning purposes, for groups of less agile dancers and to suit particular sequence dances.

Timing of the Steps

Every step in a sequence dance has a relative time length of 2, 1, ½ or ¼ beats. Although this numerical system is very clear, it is not ideal for dance scripts since fractions take up space and cause problems with verbal counting.

There are two common methods of indicating step time lengths on scripts - a numerical method using 1, 2, 3 ... and a letter system including the letters S (Slow) and Q (Quick). In both systems 'and' and 'a' are used as modifying symbols to indicate fractions of beats.

In reading scripts it is always wise to count up the number of steps in each bar and make sure that the total of the beat values is correct. If you have 3 steps in 1 bar of a foxtrot the beat lengths for all the steps should add up to 4 - if not there is an error in the script or you have made a mistake somewhere! This is particularly important with the letter notation since S = 2 beats for dances in 4/4 time but S = 1 beat for dances like the tango in 2/4 time.

Timing in Waltzes

Timing in waltzes is usually straightforward with 1 step to each beat counted as 1.2.3 for each bar.

Sometimes the weight is retained on one foot for more than 1 beat while the other foot remains stationary or is used to point, kick, flick, tap or brush. Thus the first bar of the Sweetheart Waltz is counted 1.23 (only one full stop). In more detail:-

Steps		Count
1	LF fwd down LOD	1
2	Point RF fwd	2 3

This is an example of a **hesitation** movement when progression is temporarily suspended.

A modern development in waltzes has been to make more use of figures like chassés and lock steps which involve ½ beat steps. Half beats are expressed by using the modifying word 'and' (written as '&' in the script). Thus for 1 bar of a waltz some alternative timings are:-

```
1 and 2.3        1.2 and 3        1.2.3 and
1  &  2.3        1.2  &  3        1.2.3  &
Q  Q  S S        S Q  Q  S        S S Q  Q
```

The 4th bar of the Pearl Waltz (1995) has 5 steps counted as:-

```
1.2 and 3 and
1.2  &  3  &
S Q  Q  Q  Q
```

The 'one and' is spoken more rapidly to give it the same time length as 'two' and 'three' in the verbal counting.

The term 'syncopation' is used in a broad sense in dancing to mean any departure from the normal rhythm. Thus, in the waltz chassé, 2 of the steps are taken to 1 beat of music. A syncopated figure like the syncopated weave is carried out in fewer beats than the normal waltz weave.

Step Lengths in 4/4 Time

Most sequence dances are performed to music in 4/4 time and counted in Slow-Quick notation where S (Slow) = 2 beats, Q (Quick) = 1 beat. Thus the 2 bars of the walk in the social slow foxtrot are counted as:-

```
Slow      Slow      Quick     Quick     Slow
 S         S         Q         Q         S
 2         2         1         1         2
```

Half beats are expressed using the 'and' modifier as in the waltz. An example is the 9th bar of the Queslett Quickstep (1992) which has 5 steps counted as:-

$$Q \quad Q \quad Q\& \quad Q \quad (1 \quad 1 \quad ½ \quad ½ \quad 1)$$

Numerical timings are used in the gavotte (1.2.3.4) and the cha cha cha (2.3.4&1). The rumba has a normal timing of 2.3.4 1 sometimes expressed as Q.Q.S in old scripts.

The chassé in the jive involves quarter beats using the 'a' modifier for the timing:-

```
Step        Step        Chassé
 Q           Q           QaQ
 1           1           ¾¼1
```

Step Lengths in 2/4 Time

In tango scripts S = 1 beat, Q = ½ beat (not S = 2, Q = 1 as in 4/4 time). Thus the timing for 1 bar may be:-

```
S S      QQ S      QQQQ       S Q&Q      QQ&QQ
1 1      ½½ 1      ½½½½       1 ¼¼½      ½½¼¼½
```

Some bars in sambas are counted as:-

```
        1a2      (¾¼1)
```

Step Lengths in 6/8 Time

6/8 is an example of compound duple-time. There are 2 beats in each bar, each beat being 3 x ⅛ notes (1½ crochets or 3 quavers). It is sometimes counted as though there were 6 beats in each bar. Thus the pas de basque which is a common old-time dancing figure occupies 1 bar in 6/8 time and may be counted as:-

$$1 \quad \& \quad a \quad 2 \quad \& \quad a \qquad (\text{Beats } 1 \; 2 \; 3 \; 4 \; 5 \; 6)$$

(Notice that 'a' and '&' are used to indicate beats here - not as modifiers as in previous sections.)

SOME USEFUL ADDRESSES

Suppliers of Dance Scripts

1.   North Star Publishers, P.O. Box 20, Otley, West Yorkshire, LS21 2SA. 01943 462269. Publisher of 'Sequence Dancing World' (10 issues per year). Supplier of scripts and books of scripts, etc.

2.   Brockbank Lane Sequence Script Service, P.O. Box 2341, Weymouth, Dorset, DT4 9YZ. 01305 770157. Supplier of scripts and script accessories. Many scripts have the lady's in addition to the man's steps. Revised script list available on 4 cards listing all dances issued through the script service Volumes 1-46 (1950 onwards).

3.   Northern Dance Services (NDS), 18 Commercial Street, Shipley, West Yorkshire, BD18 3SP. 01274 586829. Dance music and large collection of scripts.

Script Collections

4.   (i)   66 Modern Sequence Dances.
     (ii)   66 Old-Time Dances.
     (iii) 48 Sequence Dances compiled by Bill and May Botham in 1953.
     (iv)   Collections of scripts of winning sequence dances from 1988 onwards year by year. Available from North Star Publishers ('1' above).

5.   (i)   Modern and Latin Sequence Dances, ISTD (24 scripts).
     (ii)   Modern and Latin Sequence Dances, BCBD (32 scripts).
     (iii) Party Dances and Games, ISTD (34 scripts). Available from ISTD Sales Office, Imperial House, 22/26 Paul St., London, EC2A 4QE. 0171 377 1577.

6. 'Party Dances', Nancy Clarke (34 scripts). Available with many other books on dancing from The Ballroom Dancing Times Book and Video Service, 45-47 Clerkenwell Green, London, EC1R 0EB. 0171 250 3006.

7. 'Ken Fuller's Fun and Party Dances', Whitworth, 1996 (see inside back cover).

Suppliers of Books on Dancing

8. Dance Books Limited, 15 Cecil Court, London, WC2N 4EZ. 0171 836 2314.

9. Hearn and Spencer Limited, House of Dance, The Courtyard, Aurelia Road, Croydon, Surrey, CR0 3BF. 0181 664 8288.

Ballroom Dancing

10. Ballroom Dancing, Alex Moore, A and C Black, London, 1992.

11. Modern Ballroom Dancing, Victor Silvester, Stanley Paul, 1993.

Sequence Dancing Videos

12. 'Observe and Learn Series', 10 Volumes (5 dances per volume) of popular old-time and modern sequence dances - endorsed by The British Dance Council and the UKA. Obtainable from Westport (UK) Limited, P.O. Box 15, Keynsham, Bristol, BS18 1XU. 0117 864097/864174.

Music, Books and Videos

13. Maestro Records Limited, P.O. Box 85B, East Molesey, Surrey, KT8 9EJ. 0181 398 9018.

SECTION II

SCRIPTS OF POPULAR

SEQUENCE DANCES

This section contains full scripts of more than 30 popular sequence dances with notes on their performance; many more dances are listed in abbreviated form. The standard four ballroom dances and swings are dealt with first followed by old-time and Latin-American dances. In any chapter the dances are generally arranged in order of increasing difficulty.

Most scripts are more or less in their original format as they appear in:-

(a)   '66 Popular Modern Sequence Dances'
(b)   '66 Old Time Dances'

Both script collections may be obtained from:-

North Star Publishers, P. O. Box 20, Otley, West Yorkshire, LS21 2SA.

A few scripts have been modified to strike a balance between current practice and the intentions of the arranger.

CHAPTER 5

MODERN WALTZES

For anyone starting sequence dancing, the modern sequence waltz is a good beginning. It is performed to music in 3/4 time having 3 beats to the bar with the accent on the first beat - a rhythm that is easily counted. The tempo is relatively slow at 30-32 bpm compared with old-time (40-44 bpm) and Viennese waltzes (58-68 bpm). Most social dancers will have tried a modern waltz at one time or another.

A 'modern' waltz is not necessarily of recent origin - the Festival Waltz of 1950 is modern whereas the Magnolia Waltz arranged in 1987 is old-time. Modern dances in this sense are danced in the 'modern' style in ballroom hold with body contact being maintained at all times. They have standard dancing figures and a highly developed technique involving rise and fall, sway, footwork and contrary body movement. The five 'modern' dances are the modern waltz, foxtrot, quickstep, modern tango and Viennese waltz. The modern sequence waltz is a graceful, elegant dance - second only to the tango in popularity at the present time.

Old-time (as distinct from modern) waltzes are played at a faster tempo. Steps are taken more on the ball of the foot and the feet are closed at an angle rather than parallel. The figures have names derived from ballet like 'pas de valse' and 'glissade'. In earlier years the old-time waltz was the queen of the ballroom - one third of old-time sequence dances were waltzes and another third had old-time waltz elements. Dances in this style are discussed in a later chapter.

(Date and arranger unknown)

Start in normal ballroom hold, man facing, lady backing down LOD. Man's steps are described, lady's steps are counterpart. Tempo 30 bpm.

Bar   Count

1-8   Step Points - Clockwise Squares

| 1 | LF fwd down LOD | 1 |
| | Point RF fwd | 2 3 |

| 2 | RF fwd down LOD | 1 |
| | Point LF fwd | 2 3 |

3	LF fwd	1
	Side RF to wall	2
	Close LF to RF	3

4	RF back agst LOD	1
	Side LF to centre	2
	Close RF to LF	3

5-8   Repeat bars 1-4

There is no turn on any of these steps - the man is facing, the lady backing down LOD.

9-12   Reverse Waltz Square

9	LF fwd turning L	1
	RF to side along LOD	2
	Close LF to RF facing centre (¼ turn)	3

10	RF bk still turning L	1
	LF to side	2
	Close RF to LF now fcg agst LOD	3

11,12 Repeat bars 9 and 10 turning ¼ to L
       in each to finish facing down LOD

One complete turn is made in bars 9-12.

Although the figures in these bars are relatively simple they deserve careful study - they give practice in relating abbreviations and alignments in the scripts to the actual dancing process.

1,2   *Step, point, hesitation (repeated)*
       As with most sequence dances in ballroom hold the first step is man LF fwd, lady RF bk. The second step is to touch the RF to the floor without weight (ww). The position is held for the third beat - the hesitation.
       Bar 2 is a repeat of bar 1 on opposite feet.

3,4   *Clockwise square*
       Bar 3 is a **LF forward closed change** - forward, side, close like an inverted letter 'L'.
       Bar 4 is the **RF backward closed change** - back, side and close. The two figures together make an **amalgamation** called the **clockwise square**.

5-8   *Bars 1-4 repeated* - step and point twice followed by another clockwise square.

9-12   *Reverse waltz square*
       Unlike the clockwise squares of bars 3 and 4 there is a turning action and the man's feet do not always face down LOD.
       Bars 9 and 11 involve ¼ turns to the L (2 forward steps and close with turn). They can be seen as **forward closed changes** with a turn or as **1-3 reverse turns underturned** from ⅜ to ¼.
       Bars 10 and 12 are the corresponding backward turns (backward closed changes with a turn or 4-6 reverse turns underturned). There is a complete turn in this square in which the man faces down LOD, C, agst LOD, W and down LOD again.

13-16 Forward Steps - Check - Backward Steps
- Side Hover to Whisk - Close

13	LF, RF, LF fwd down LOD. Check	123
14	RF, LF, RF bk agst LOD	123
15	LF to side with hover action	1
	Replace weight to RF	2
	Cross LF behind RF (Whisk)	3
16	RF fwd (small step)	1
	LF to side	2
	Close RF to LF	3

SWEETHEART WALTZ   NOTES ON BARS 13-16

13,14 *Forward walks, check, backward walks*
Three forward walks LRL followed by 3 backward walks RLR. The check in between is the change of direction between these movements (often carried out with a flexing of the knee - plié).

15,16 *Side hover, whisk, close*
The side hover of the first 2 steps is a rock action with a transfer of weight from RF to LF and back again; it is performed with a floating action rising on the toes. The final step of bar 15 is cross LF behind RF - a common action in whisks.
(A variation is for the man to turn L leading the lady into fallaway position with both facing C.)
Bar 16 is a modified RF fwd closed change moving to side to regain starting position.

Summary of the Sweetheart Waltz

Step, point, hesitate (twice). Clockwise square. Step, point, hesitate (twice). Clockwise square. Reverse waltz square (4 x ¼ turns to L). 3 forward steps, check, 3 backward steps. Side hover, whisk, step, closed finish.

WALTZ MARIE

This dance is sometimes said to be the most popular sequence dance of all time. It is one of the few modern (slow tempo) waltzes to be performed at old-time sessions - it was the only modern waltz to appear on Harry Davidson's BBC programme 'Those were the days' (1943 onwards).

Unfortunately, it is danced in different ways in different regions leading to confusion. Many dancers maintain that a sequence should be performed exactly as the arranger intended it to be. There is some merit in this point of view but with older dances things are not always that simple. As a learner it is prudent to follow the majority!

Mr. J. Senior of Stretford arranged the dance in 1948; he was not a professional but a keen amateur sequence dancer with a partiality for the modern style. His friend, Len Meadows, gave the dance considerable publicity in the Manchester region and it was an immediate success. Many local MC's 'poached' it for their clubs after having seen it on only one occasion and inevitably various versions emerged. Mr. Senior was no script writer and he invited Bill Botham to script the dance to reduce the confusion. This revised script eventually appeared in Bill Botham's weekly feature 'On With The Dance' in the 'Manchester City News'. The dance aroused great interest and many professionals and 'experts' suggested changes. One southern dance teacher proposed a lady's allemande in bars 11 and 12 to make the dance more acceptable to old-time dancers. Mr. Senior compromised on certain points and Bill Botham modified the original script to produce the 'authentic' version - included in Bill Botham's MC's handbook of 1953 (see page 45). The script which follows is a modern version arranged by Michael Gwynne.

Ballroom hold, man facing, lady backing LOD. Man's steps described.   Lady dances counterpart unless otherwise stated. Tempo 32 bpm.

Bar   Count

1-4   Reverse Turns
1   LF fwd turning L   1
         Side RF across LOD (wide step moving   2
         well round partner)
         Close LF to RF parallel position,   3
         now bkg DW down LOD
2   RF bk turning L   1
         Side LF   2
         Close RF to LF parallel position,   3
         now facing DW against LOD
3   LF fwd DW agst LOD   1
         Side RF   2
         Close LF to RF to end fcg DW   3
4   RF bk DC agst LOD   1
         Side LF toe pointing down LOD   2
         Close RF to LF to end fcg down LOD   3

5-8   Forward Change - Pivots and Feather
5   LF fwd down LOD   1
         Side RF and slightly fwd   2
         Close LF to RF parallel position   3
6   RF fwd dn LOD pivoting strongly to   1
         R at end of step almost bkg LOD
         LF bk down LOD   2
         Continue turning R trans wt to RF   3
         moving it sltly R to face down LOD
7   LF bk agst LOD   1
         RF bk agst LOD   2
         Side LF fcg DC down LOD preparing to   3
         step outside partner
8   RF fwd DC down LOD on lady's R   1
         LF fwd down LOD   2
         RF fwd DW on R side of lady; curving   3
         ¼ turn to R in this bar (feather)

1-4   *Reverse turns*

A complete turn to the left to regain the original alignment of facing down LOD. These reverse turns resemble the reverse square in the Sweetheart Waltz but the angles of turn are ⅜, ¼, ¼, ⅛ instead of ¼, ¼, ¼, ¼ (the original script has turns of ½, 0, ½, 0). What many dancers do is to keep turning left through various angles depending on the proximity of other dancers and corner situations and use the final 3 steps to make sure that they finish facing down LOD.

5   *Left foot forward closed change*

This changes the leading foot from LF to RF preparing for the natural turn of bar 6.

6   *Stationary pivots (natural pivot turn)*

This is an unusual type of turn in modern waltzes which involves a complete turn to the right over 3 steps. (The normal waltz natural turn is ⅜ over 3 steps.) It is a full continuous body turn to the R consisting of a RF pivot, LF bk and another RF pivot with the RF remaining almost in the same place. This turn is very similar to the propelled pivot turn used in old-time dancing, e.g. old versions of the Lancers.

7,8   *Backward walks, side step, feather*

LF bk, RF bk followed by LF to side turning ⅛ to face DC preparing to step outside partner.

Bar 8 is 3 forward walks RF, LF, RF outside partner curving ¼ to R. (This resembles the feather step of the slow foxtrot with a different timing of 1.2.3.)

9-12   Whisk-Whisk Wing-Lady Reverse Allemande

9	LF fwd DW square to lady	1

9   LF fwd DW square to lady   1
    Side RF across LOD tng to face DC   2
    (¼ turn to L), leading partner to PP
    Cross LF in behind RF, end PP fcg C   3
10   RF fwd towards C turning R   1
    Side LF and diag bk fcg LOD   2
    Cross RF behind LF fcg DW ending   3
    with lady on L side, man ¼ turn to R,
    (lady no turn)
11   LF fwd release hold of RH and comm   1
    tng lady L under raised hands
    RF diag fwd (medium step)   2
    Close LF to RF in parallel position   3
12   RF fwd still turning lady to L   1
    LF diag fwd   2
    Close RF to LF - end square to   3
    partner taking up ballroom hold

13-16 Turning Forward Changes - Reverse Turn

13   LF fwd DW turning L   1
    Side RF across LOD   2
    Close LF to RF parallel position   3
    rising to toes with foot and body rise
    (¼ turn to L in this bar)
14   RF fwd DC OP on R side turning to R   1
    LF to side across LOD   2
    Close RF to LF parallel position   3
    rising to toes with foot and body rise
    (¼ turn to R in this bar)
15   LF fwd DW turning L on L side ptnr   1
    Side RF   2
    Close LF to RF parallel position; fcg   3
    DC with partners square (¼ turn to
    L in this bar)
16   RF bk DW agst LOD, no turn   1
    Side LF   2
    Close RF to LF parallel position   3
    (No turn in bar 16, fcg DC throughout)

9,10   *Whisk-whisk wing*
Bar 9 is a forward whisk with a ¼ turn left finishing in PP. Bar 10 is a similar movement on opposite feet turning right and leading the lady to the left side for the following turn. (Lady: LF fwd, RF fwd, LF fwd to L of partner - wing - no turn.)

11,12 *LF and RF closed changes (lady reverse allemande)*
The man takes 6 steps: LF fwd, RF to side, close, RF fwd, LF to side, close, moving DW; turning the lady into a solo reverse turn under raised hands - man's LH holds lady's RH (allemande).

13,14 *LF and RF turning forward changes*
These are saunter-type figures described in the original script as L and R swivels.

15,16 *Reverse turn with closed finish*
Bar 15 is an underturned reverse turn finishing facing DC (a ¼ turn).
Bar 16 is a right foot backward closed change without turn.

In Bill Botham's script there are differences in the reverse turns in bars 1-4 and there is a solo turn instead of an allemande for the lady in bars 11 and 12.

Summary of the Waltz Marie

Two reverse turns. Fwd change. Stationary pivots on RF making a full turn to R (RF pivot, LF back, RF pivot). Curving feather. Whisks to R and L (lady wing). Step, step, close, repeated moving DW (Lady: allemande under man's LH). Two forward swivels. Quarter reverse turn with closed finish.

WALTZ CATHRINE (OR CATHERINE)

This modern waltz written by Arthur Shaw of Sheffield in 1956 is still popular - particularly with winter sun dancers in Benidorm!

WALTZ CATHRINE   DANCE SCRIPT BARS 1-8

Normal ballroom hold, man facing, lady backing down LOD. Man's steps given, lady's steps are counterpart except where otherwise stated. Tempo 30 bpm.

Bar		Count
1-4	**Reverse Turn and Back Change Repeated**	
1	LF fwd comm to turn L	1
	RF to side across LOD (bkg DW)	2
	Close LF to RF bkg LOD	3
2	RF bk down LOD	1
	LF to side	2
	Close RF to LF fcg agst LOD	3
3,4	Repeat steps of bars 3 and 4 to end fcg LOD preparing to step DW outside ptnr	
5-8	**Forward Passing Change - 123 Natural Turn - Natural Spin Turn with Closed Finish**	
5	LF fwd diag to wall	1
	RF fwd outside partner on R	2
	(R hip to R hip)	
	LF fwd	3
6	RF fwd comm to turn R	1
	LF to side across LOD	2
	Close RF to LF bkg LOD (lady fcg LOD)	3
7	LF bk turning strongly R with RF	1
	held in CBMP (½ turn approx.)	
	RF fwd down LOD still turning (pivot)	2
	LF to side and slightly bk fcg down	3
	LOD (Lady: RF diag fwd DC agst LOD)	
8	RF bk agst LOD	1
	LF to side	2
	Close RF to LF fcg down LOD	3

1-4   *Rotary reverse turn, back change repeated*
A rotary reverse turn through ½ is followed by a backward closed change without turn; these figures are then repeated. This achieves the same result as the reverse square (see bars 9-12 of the Sweetheart Waltz) but the dancers turn through ½,0,½,0 giving a narrow rectangle rather than the ¼,¼,¼,¼ of the reverse square.

In dances of this kind which include a complete reverse turn over 4 bars, most dancers steer a middle course. They turn left through various angles in each bar depending on proximity to other dancers and corners, using the final turn to make sure they have the correct alignment.

5   *Forward passing change*
The 3 forward steps on partner's R side change the leading foot to the RF preparing for the natural turn that is to follow.

In recent waltzes the LF closed change is usually preferred (step, step, side close).

6-8   *Natural spin turn with closed finish*
This is one of the most popular of waltz turns - it is repeated in bars 12 and 13 followed by outside checks.

The **full natural spin turn** has 6 steps - 123 of the natural turn (bar 6) followed by one pivot step and two spin steps.

The pivot step is a LF backward step with a strong turn to the right with the RF held out in front (in CBMP). This is followed by spins on RF and LF to complete the turn.

The closed finish of bar 8 is a RF backward closed change - RF bk, LF to side and close without turn.

9-12   Whisk - Wing - Closed Telemark - 123 Natural Turn

9	LF fwd down LOD	1
	RF to side to wall	2
	Cross LF behind RF (whisk)	3

10	RF fwd	1
	Close LF to RF without weight	2 3
	(Lady takes 3 steps L, R, L round	
	man on his left side - wing)	

11	LF fwd DC on lady's L side turning L	1
	RF to side across LOD still turning	2
	LF to side down LOD, now facing DW	3

12	RF fwd comm to turn R	1
	LF to side across LOD	2
	Close RF to LF to end bkg LOD	3

13-16 Natural Spin Turn - Checks to L and R - Closed Finish

13	LF bk turning strongly R with RF	1
	held in CBMP (½ turn approx.)	
	RF fwd down LOD still turning (pivot)	2
	LF to side and slightly back fcg LOD	3
	(Lady: RF diag fwd DC agst LOD)	

14	RF bk in CBMP turning L to face DC	1
	LF to side still turning	2
	RF fwd DC on lady's R side (check)	3

15	LF bk in CBMP turning R to face DW	1
	RF to side still turning	2
	LF fwd DW on lady's L side (check)	3

16	RF bk turning L to face down LOD	1
	LF to side	2
	Close RF to LF to end facing LOD	3

9,10   *Whisk, wing*

The **forward whisk** of bar 9 moves the partners into PP both with feet crossed (the lady turns ¼ on steps 1 and 2). In the **wing** of bar 10 the man leads the lady strongly forward on step 1 and slowly closes LF to RF without weight on steps 2 and 3. (Lady: LF, RF, LF fwd curving strongly L preparing to step OP.)

11   *Closed telemark turn*

This often follows a whisk and wing. It is a compact turn through a large angle (often ¾) widely used in the slow foxtrot and other dances. The man swivels first on the LF then on the RF; it is more or less a spot turn with man's and lady's feet close together. (An open telemark turn would finish in promenade position.)

12,13 *Natural spin turn* - As in bars 6 and 7.

14,15 *Checks to R and L of lady*

The weight is transferred to the leading foot and then replaced to the back foot (checking action). Checks on either side of the lady with a step or a chassé in between occur in many sequence dances.

16   *Closed finish*

A RF backward closed change with ¼ turn to L sometimes called a 456 reverse turn (bar 8 with ¼ turn to L).

Summary of the Waltz Cathrine

Rotary reverse turn, closed change repeated (often danced as a waltz square), 3 forward steps leading to a natural spin turn with closed finish. Whisk, wing and closed telemark. Natural spin turn. Checks to L and R side of lady. Closed finish.

WOODSIDE WALTZ   DANCE SCRIPT BARS 1-8
Arranged by J. Fanning in 1964

Commence in ballroom hold, man facing DW. Man's steps described. Lady dances counterpart unless otherwise stated. Tempo 32 bpm.

Bar   Count

1-4   Closed Change - Natural Spin Turn - Turning Lock

1	LF fwd DW	1
	Side RF and slightly fwd	2
	Close LF to RF	3
2	RF fwd turning R	1
	Side LF still turning	2
	Close RF to LF to end bkg LOD	3
3	LF bk dn LOD and pivot half turn R	1
	RF fwd in CBMP still tng, fcg LOD	2
	Side LF and slightly bk, bkg DC	3
4	Back RF, R shoulder leading	1
	Cross LF in front of RF	2
	RF bk and slightly R, turning to L	&
	Side LF and slightly fwd ptg DW	3

5-8   Hesitation Change - Reverse Turn

5	Fwd RF in CBMP, OP DW, turning R	1
	Side LF still turning	2
	Close RF to LF to end bkg LOD	3
6	LF back turning R	1
	Side RF small step, fcg DC	2
	Brush LF to RF ww (heel pull)	3
7	LF fwd DC turning L	1
	Side RF still turning	2
	Close LF to RF to end bkg LOD	3
8	RF bk turning L	1
	Side LF, toe ptg DW	2
	Close RF to LF fcg DW	3

1,2   *LF closed change*
      The step, step, close of bar 1 change the leading foot from LF to RF to prepare for the 123 natural turn of bar 2.

3,4   *Natural spin turn, turning lock*
      Following the natural turn of bar 2 the LF is pulled back pivoting on the heel and turning strongly R with the RF held out in front.   Weight is then transferred to the RF continuing to turn (see Waltz Cathrine).
      Bar 4 is the turning lock - it is a backward lock step (feet crossed) followed by ¼ turn to the L on the next step.   Notice that it is a syncopated figure - 4 steps in the bar timed SQQS.

5,6   *Hesitation change*
      Bar 5 is 123 of the natural turn (see bar 2) but started outside partner.   It is followed by the heel pull - the man steps back with his LF turning R and slowly pulls his RF to it.   After a slight hesitation he moves into the reverse turn of bars 7 and 8. The hesitation change is a rapid method of moving from a natural to a reverse turn.

7,8   *1-6 reverse turn*
      The standard waltz reverse turn (starting with feet together facing DC, finishing with feet together facing DW - ¾ turn to L).

Summary of the Woodside Waltz

Closed change. Natural spin turn. Turning lock. Hesitation change. Reverse turn. Whisk. Wing. Open telemark. Hover in PP. Contra check. Natural turn to fallaway whisk. Closed finish.

Bar		Count

9-12 Whisk - Wing - Open Telemark - Promenade Hover

9	LF fwd DW, turning to L	1
	RF diag fwd, R shoulder ldg	2
	Cross LF behind RF in PP fcg DC	3
10	RF fwd and across in PP and CBMP ptg DC, body fcg LOD	1
	Comm close LF to RF, body turning L	2
	Close LF to RF ww, body turning L (Lady: wing)	3
11	LF fwd in CBMP OP on L side DC tng L	1
	RF to side bkg DW, still turning (Lady: heel turn)	2
	Side LF and sltly fwd in PP along LOD, toe ptg DW, body fcg wall	3
12	Fwd RF and across in PP and CBMP along LOD tng R	1
	Side LF fcg wall	2
	Rise higher on toes and transfer wt to RF fcg DW agst LOD (Lady: no turn)	3

13-16 Contra Check - Natural Turn to Fallaway Whisk - Closed Finish

13	LF fwd in CBMP DW agst LOD body turning L and knees slightly flexed	1
	Transfer wt bk to RF turning L	2
	Side LF ptg DW	3
14	RF fwd in CBMP OP DW turning R	1
	Side LF still turning	2
	Close RF to LF to end bkg LOD	3
15	LF back turning R	1
	Side RF and slightly bk turning partner to fallaway position	2
	Cross LF loosely behind RF in fallaway position facing DC	3
16	RF fwd and across in CBMP and PP tng R	1
	Side LF turning square to partner	2
	Close RF to LF fcg DW	3

9,10   *Whisk, wing*

The forward whisk is a triangular movement for the man ending with feet crossed in promenade position. In the wing the man leads his partner forward to his L side and slowly closes his LF to his RF on steps 2 and 3. (The lady walks round the man taking 3 forward steps L, R, L curving strongly to the L and finishing bkg DC.)

11,12   *Open telemark and hover*

The man turns strongly to his L on his LF then swivels on the ball of his RF moving his LF along the line of dance in PP. (Lady: RF back tng L and closing LF to RF in parallel position - a **heel turn**; the RF is then moved forward down LOD in PP.) The hover in PP of bar 12 is a checking movement carried out with a floating action in which the weight is transferred from one to the other moving on the toes.

13   *Contra check*

This is a rocking action involving a check forward on the LF flexing the knees. Weight is transferred to the RF on the second step followed by a side step turning ¼ to the L preparing for the natural turn which is to follow.

14-16   *Natural turn, fallaway whisk, closed finish*

Bar 14 is the 123 natural turn starting outside partner. This is followed by a turning backward movement into fallaway finishing with LF crossed behind RF. Bar 16 is a RF forward closed change with a ¼ turn to the R.

For a summary of the Woodside Waltz see page 63.

EMMERDALE WALTZ

This modern waltz arranged by W. J. Crook contains some old-time elements, notably the solo turns and the hover and whisk in double hold.

EMMERDALE WALTZ **DANCE SCRIPT**
BARS 1-8

Ballroom hold, man facing LOD. Man's steps described. Lady dances counterpart unless otherwise stated. Tempo 31 bpm.

Bar		Count
1-4	**Reverse Square**	
1	LF fwd DC	1
	RF to side	2
	Close LF to RF to face centre	3
2	RF bk down LOD	1
	LF to side	2
	Close RF to LF to end fcg agst LOD	3
3,4	Repeat bars 1 and 2 agst LOD to finish fcg down LOD	
5-8	**Step and Point in line - Step and Point in PP - Solo Turn - Promenade Hover**	
5	LF fwd along LOD	1
	Point RF fwd in line with partner	2 3
6	RF fwd DW starting to turn to PP	1
	Point LF to side along LOD in PP releasing hold	2 3
7	LF fwd DC along LOD turning to L	1
	RF to side still turning	2
	Back LF along LOD to end fcg wall	3
8	Cross RF over LF fcg DW taking up double hold (man's LH holds lady's RH, man's RH holds lady's LH)	1
	Side LF along LOD	2
	Replace weight to RF with hover action turning to face wall and partner	3

1-4   *Reverse square*
Four reverse turns of ¼ with feet closed on every third step completing a full turn to the original position after the 4 bars (Sweetheart Waltz bars 9-12).

5,6   *Step and point in line, step and point in PP*
After the LF has moved forward the RF is brought up to it and the floor is touched with the toe with the instep fully arched (no transfer of weight at this stage). After a hesitation of 1 beat the RF is moved forward and the LF used to point turning into PP. (Compare bars 1 and 2 of the Sweetheart Waltz.)

7   *Open turn*
The hold is released for the man to do a solo telemark turn to the L while the lady does the corresponding turn to the R. Both turn outwards in opposite directions to end facing one another.

8   *Promenade hover*
The partners take up double hold - man's L hand in lady's R hand, man's R hand in lady's L hand (old-time hold no. 5). The man moves down the LOD in PP crossing his RF over his LF turning R and moving his LF to the side to face DW. He then transfers his weight back to the RF with a hover action in PP.

The hover is a type of rock with elevation of the body and sway to produce a floating action. Notice that in this hover dancers are in counter promenade position (CPP) - promenade position with man's and lady's positions interchanged.

Bar   Count

9-12   **Fallaway Whisk - Wing - Open Telemark - Promenade Hover**

Bar		Count
9	Cross LF over RF	1
	(Lady: RF over LF)	
	RF to side agst LOD to face wall	2
	Cross LF behind RF (whisk position)	3
	to end fcg DW in PP	
10	RF fwd DW taking up ballroom hold	1
	Close LF to RF ww counting 2,3	2 3
	(Lady: 3 curving steps to L crossing	
	over in front of man - wing)	
11	LF fwd DC with strong turn to L	1
	RF to side with strong turn to L	2
	swivelling on ball of RF	
	LF fwd along LOD in PP	3
	(Lady: heel turn)	
12	RF fwd DW along LOD	1
	LF to side along LOD, hover action	2
	Replace weight to RF turning	3
	partner square	

13-16   **Contra check - Half Natural Turn - Natural Spin Turn**

Bar		Count
13	LF fwd sq to partner fcg DW agst LOD	1
	Replace weight to RF	2
	LF to side along LOD	3
14	RF fwd DW on R side partner tng R	1
	LF to side along LOD still turning	2
	Close RF to LF, bkg down LOD	3
15	LF back along LOD in CBMP tng R	1
	Extend RF fwd turning R	2
	LF side to C	3
16	RF back agst LOD	1
	LF to side to C	2
	Close RF to LF to restart	3

9   *Fallaway whisk*

The man moves his LF forward turning inwards (to L) and brings his RF to the side still turning; he crosses his LF behind his RF on the third step in PP facing DW (a fallaway whisk), adopting ballroom hold. (Fallaway position is like PP but the partners are moving backwards; the angle apart is slightly greater.)

10   *Wing*

The man moves his RF forward DW leading the lady to his L side. He then closes his LF to his RF without weight and hesitates. (Lady: LF, RF, LF curving strongly L to check on man's L side.)

11,12   *Open telemark, promenade hover*

The open telemark is a compact turn through a large angle to the L finishing in PP. (The lady moves her RF back DC and then closes her LF to her RF to perform a **heel turn**; this is followed by a RF fwd step in PP facing DC.) The promenade hover is a repeat of bar 8 in ballroom hold.

13-16   *Contra check, natural spin turn*

Bar 13 is the contra check. The body turns L on step 1, R on step 2. The final side step prepares for the spin turns of bars 14-16 (123 natural turn, pivot and spin steps, closed finish - see bars 6,7,8 of the Waltz Cathrine).

Summary of the Emmerdale Waltz

Reverse square. 2 step points. Outward solo turns. Hover and fallaway whisk (in double hold). Wing. Open telemark, hover, contra check. Natural spin turn with closed finish.

*Start in ballroom hold with man facing, lady backing DC.
Man's steps described, lady dances counterpart unless
otherwise stated. Tempo 32 bpm.*

Bar   Count

1-4   Reverse Turn - Whisk - Chassé in PP

Bar		Count
1	Fwd LF, comm turn L	1
	Side RF still turning L	2
	Close LF to RF now backing LOD	3
2	Back RF down LOD, comm turn L	1
	Side LF still turning L	2
	Close RF to LF now fcg diag to wall	3
3	Fwd LF DW comm turn L	1
	RF diag fwd, R shoulder leading	2
	Cross LF behind RF tng ptnr into PP	3
	now fcg LOD preparing to move DC	
4	Fwd RF and across in CBMP & PP mvg DC	1
	Side LF and slightly fwd in PP	2
	Close RF to LF in PP	&
	Side LF and slightly fwd in PP	3

**5-8   Half Reverse Weave - Back Lock - Open
Impetus - Left Foot Whisk**

Bar		Count
5	Fwd RF and across in CBMP and PP tng L	1
	Fwd LF to C	2
	Side RF and sltly bk, now bkg DW	3
6	LF bk moving DW, leading lady to	1
	step fwd outside on R	
	RF bk	2
	Cross LF in front of RF	&
	RF diag bk	3
7	LF bk comm turn R (Lady: fwd OP)	1
	Close RF to LF (heel tn) still tng R	2
	LF diag fwd in PP, L shldr ldg fcg	3
	DW preparing to move along LOD	
8	Fwd RF & across in CBMP & PP along LOD	1
	Side LF and sltly fwd, tng lady sq	2
	Cross RF behind LF, leading lady to	3
	step back into whisk position	

1,2   *Full reverse turn*
A 123 forward reverse turn followed by a 456 backward waltz reverse turn.   Notes and foot diagram appear on pages 28-30.

3   *Whisk*
Compare bar 15 of the Sweetheart Waltz and bar 9 of the Emmerdale Waltz.   The bar finishes with man's LF crossed behind his RF (lady opposite).

4   *Chassé from promenade position* (see p. 35)
Taken in PP moving DC.   The 4 steps are counted SQQS; feet are closed on 3rd step.

5   *Half reverse weave*
A quarter turn to the left moving from PP into line. This is a waltz reverse turn in which the feet do not close; it often follows an open impetus turn

6   *Back lock*
A backward chassé step (compare bar 4) taken backwards with feet crossed and partner on R side (a syncopated step).

7   *Open impetus turn*
The man moves his LF back turning R and closes his RF to it still turning with transfer of weight (a heel turn) - a popular figure in foxtrots and quicksteps.   ('Open' here means finishing in PP.)

8   *Left whisk*
Sometimes called a contra whisk; often followed (as here) by a twist turn.   Man steps RF fwd in PP, then LF to side and crosses RF behind LF with a body turn to L.   (The lady's steps are LF fwd, RF to side and slightly back, LF bk with a total turn of ⅜ to the L - she unwinds the man.)

Bar   Count

**9-12 Twist Turn R - Hover - Back Half Reverse
Turn - Travelling Contra Check**

9   Twist to R on both feet tng approx ¾   1
         to R ending bkg DW agst LOD ending   2
         with wt on RF (lady walks round   3
         man R,L,R,L to end fcg DW agst LOD)

10   LF bk comm turn R, leading lady to   1
         step fwd outside on R side
         RF to side and sltly fwd still tng and   2
         brushing LF twds RF (lady now in line)
         LF bk now bkg DC (hover action)   3

11   RF bk comm turn L   1
         Side LF still turning L   2
         Close RF to LF now facing DW   3

12   LF fwd and well across body in CBMP   1
         with check action
         RF to side and sltly fwd (ss) tng to R   2
         Side LF in PP, body fcg W moving DW   3

13-16 Hover to Natural Fallaway - Hesitation Turn

13   RF fwd & across in PP & CBMP comm tn R   1
         LF diag fwd, L shoulder leading in PP,   2
         still turning R, rising on to toes
         RF bk in fallaway moving DC and   3
         bkg LOD (hover in PP)

14   LF bk in CBMP and fallaway position   1
         moving DC, starting to turn L
         RF bk to C leading lady to step in line   2
         (lady turns strongly L and slips LF
         fwd in line with partner - slip pivot)
         Side LF and slightly fwd ptg DW   3

15   RF fwd in CBMP OP comm turning R   1
         Side LF still turning R   2
         Close RF to LF, now backing LOD   3

16   Back LF down LOD comm turning R   1
         Side RF ss (heel pull), now fcg DC   2
         Brush LF to RF without weight   3

9,11   *Natural twist turn, hover, 456 reverse turn*
      The lady unwinds the man's crossed feet by taking
      4 curving steps to the R (R,L,R,L timed SQQS).
      In bar 10 the man leads the lady to step outside on
      his R and they perform a hover on the last 2 steps.
      Bar 11 is a ¼ turn to L finishing with feet closed -
      often called a closed finish. A common mistake is
      to hurry these 3 bars - there is ample time.

12   *Travelling contra check*
      This figure moves the partners **forward** into PP.
      Step 2 is RF to side and slightly fwd (small step).
      (In the ordinary contra check this step is 'replace
      weight to RF'.)

13,14 *Natural fallaway (lady slip pivot)*
      Both partners take 2 forward steps turning strongly
      R then 2 steps back in fallaway position (PP with
      a larger angle). The lady now takes 2 steps
      pivoting strongly L to face the man (slip pivot) - a
      most elegant figure.

15,16 *Natural hesitation turn*
      Bar 15 is 123 natural turn. Bar 16 is LF bk
      followed by RF to side (heel pull). The last step
      is a hesitation as LF closes to RF without weight.
      (The reverse part of this turn is bars 1 and 2 of the
      next sequence.)

Summary of the Engagement Waltz

Reverse turn. Whisk. Chassé in PP. Weave. Back lock.
Open impetus. Twist turn. Hover. 456 reverse turn.
Travelling contra check. Hover to fallaway (lady - slip
pivot). Natural hesitation turn.

SUMMARIES OF OTHER POPULAR WALTZES

Waltz Louise (1989)

Neil and Leslie Marshall, 1st SDTA

Ballroom hold facing DC. Tempo 30 bpm.

Bars

1-4	123 reverse turn. Outside check. Back lock. Outside change with reverse cross.
5-8	Drag hesitation. Back lock. Open impetus. Outside check.
9-12	Closed reverse wing with man's forward twinkle. Progressive chassé. 123 natural turn. Open impetus.
13-16	Weave from PP to PP. Chair. Slip pivot. Change of direction.

Westlynn Waltz (1990)

Howard and Joanne Cookson, 1st BATD

Ballroom hold facing DC. Tempo 30 bpm.

Bars

1-4	1.2 reverse turn. Checks to R and L of lady. Progressive chassé.
5-8	1.2 natural turn. Back lock. Closed impetus turn. 456 reverse turn.
9-12	Hover to PP. Fallaway. Slip pivot. 1.2 natural turn.
13-16	Back whisk. Wing. Curved three step. 456 reverse turn.

Crinoline Waltz (1966)

Ballroom hold, man facing LOD. Tempo 31 bpm.

Bars

1-4	Open reverse turn. Open finish. Checks to either side. Closed finish.
5-8	Repeat bars 1-4. Commence LF against LOD, finish facing LOD.
9-12	Reverse turn. Whisk. 123 weave from PP.
13-16	456 weave from PP. Natural spin turn. 456 reverse turn.

Waltz Babette (1968)
Arthur Lightfoot, 3rd OBBD, Leeds

Ballroom hold, man facing DW. Tempo 31 bpm.

Bars

1-4	Forward change. Open impetus turn. 3 of weave.
5-8	Natural turn to PP. Chair to syncopated twinkle. Forward change. 123 reverse turn.
9-12	Viennese turn. Outside check. Chassé to right. Pivot to back lock.
13-16	Outside change. Natural spin turn. 456 reverse turn underturned.

Bluebird Waltz (1982)
Michael Davies, 1st ISDC

Ballroom hold, man facing DW. Tempo 30 bpm.

Bars

1-4	Whisk. Wing. Check. Hover.
5-8	Back lock. Open impetus turn. Hover.
9-12	Same foot lunge. Hairpin run. Hesitation change.
13-16	Reverse turn. Reverse corté. Check. Spin and side close.

Honeysuckle Waltz (1985)
Graham and Avril Watkins, 1st Butlins, Pwllheli

Ballroom hold, man facing DC. Tempo 31 bpm.

Bars

1-4	Reverse turn. Whisk. Wing.
5-8	2-5 weave. Chassé from PP. Open impetus turn.
9-12	Hover. Back Hover. Swivel. Chassé from PP.
13-16	Open impetus turn. Chassé from PP. Chair. Slip pivot.

Waltz Clinique (1991)

David Hipshaw and Pauline Griffiths, 1st ADA

Ballroom hold, man facing DW. Tempo 30 bpm.

Bars

1-4	Closed change. Natural spin turn. Turning lock. Double cross.
5-8	Hinge. Recover to PP. Weave from PP.
9-12	123 natural turn. Open impetus. Tipple chassé in PP (lady wing).
13-16	Progressive chassé to R. Back lock. Closed impetus turn. 456 reverse turn underturned.

Apple Blossom Waltz (1992)

Samantha Haywood, 1st ISTD

Normal ballroom hold, man fcg DW. Tempo 31 bpm.

Bars

1-4	Whisk. Chassé in PP. Check. Slip pivot. Half reverse turn.
5-8	1-3 reverse corté. Back hover. Wing. Open telemark.
9-12	Hover from PP. Contra check to PP. Curve. Open impetus turn.
13-16	Chassé in PP. Check. Slip pivot. Reverse turn.

Denverdale Waltz (1992)

Steven and Diane Shaw, 1st Butlins, Pwllheli

Ballroom hold, man facing DC. Tempo 31 bpm.

Bars

1-4	123 reverse turn. Progressive chassé. Natural spin turn (underturned).
5-8	Outside checks to R and L. Hesitation swivel. Back lock.
9-12	Open impetus. Left whisk. Twist turn. Travelling contra check.
13-16	Weave from PP. Curved feather. 4-6 hesitation change.

OVERVIEW

All the modern sequence waltzes described in the preceding pages have certain common features in that they:-

- are played to music in 3/4 time within a tempo range of 30-32 bpm;
- start in ballroom hold;
- commence with man LF fwd, lady RF bk.

1.   Ballroom Hold

In all except two of the dances ballroom hold is maintained at all times although the partners may be square to one another or in promenade, fallaway or outside position.

(The Waltz Marie has a solo turn or allemande in bars 11, 12; the Emmerdale Waltz has solo turns in bar 7 and bars 8-9 in double hold.)

2.   Starting Foot

In nearly all sequence dances starting in **ballroom hold** the man's first step is **LF fwd** (one exception is the Aurora Foxtrot (1989) - LF bk).

When Thoinot Arbeau (1589) was asked why men started marching on the left foot his reply was, "Because most men are right footed and the left foot is weaker, so if it should come about that the left foot were to falter for any reason the right foot would be immediately ready to support it."

The lady's corresponding step is almost always 'RF bk' - perhaps it is the man's privilege to support her if she falters!

3.   **Starting Alignment**

Three alignments are used for starting modern sequence waltzes (see page 37).

Down LOD - earlier dances such as the Sweetheart, Cathrine and Crinoline waltzes.

Diagonal to Centre (DC) - waltzes starting with a figure turning left such as the reverse turn - Engagement, Westlynn and Denverdale waltzes.

Diagonal to Wall (DW) - used for waltzes in which a natural turn is imminent. The Woodside Waltz and Waltz Clinique start with a LF forward closed change followed by a natural spin turn.

4.   **Figures Used in Other Dances**

The following figures are common to the waltz, foxtrot and quickstep:-

- Impetus/telemark turns (open and closed)
- Double reverse spin
- Passing natural turn (feet pass instead of being closed in parallel position)
- Outside spin
- Outside change
- Progressive chassés (not the slow foxtrot)
- Whisk
- Fallaway reverse and slip pivot

The use of the same figure in several different dances should be a source of encouragement to the aspiring sequence dancer - having learned the impetus turn in the waltz, the same figure (possibly with a different timing) will crop up in other dances.

5.   **Reverse Square (or Two Full Reverse Turns)**

Some early waltzes start with 4 bars of reverse turns making a complete turn which brings the partners back to their original positions. The angle of turn in each bar is not the same for all waltzes.

Waltzes	Angles of turn
Emmerdale	¼, ¼, ¼, ¼
Sweetheart (bars 9-12)	¼, ¼, ¼, ¼
Marie	⅜, ¼, ¼, ⅛
Cathrine, Marie (old script)	½, 0, ½, 0

The waltz reverse square (4 x ¼ turns) moves the dancers too far into the centre of the room and this causes problems in a long narrow dancing area. At the other extreme ½,0,½,0 involves rotary half turns which are not easy to perform with elegance. In practice many dancers perform the reverse turns in the same way for all these waltzes - they keep turning left avoiding other dancers as best they can using their final turn to achieve the correct orientation for the following figure. This is a case where dancing figures are more useful than scripts - if the dance leader calls out "Two Reverse Turns", this sums up the situation in a nutshell.

Starting sequence waltzes with two reverse turns has now gone out of fashion - even starting with one complete reverse turn is less common. The last three steps (4,5,6) are often replaced by the progressive chassé as in the Denverdale Waltz.

The progressive chassé is similar to the 4-6 reverse turn but has 2 quick steps and an extra side step at the end; the timing is 1.2&3 (Slow, Quick, Quick, Slow).

6.   **Syncopated Figures**

Variety can be introduced into sequence waltzes by using figures in which 2 steps are taken to 1 beat of the music as in chassés and lock steps (see quickstep chapter). Instead of 3 steps for a bar there may be 4 steps timed 1&2.3 (QQSS), 1.2&3 (SQQS) or sometimes 1.2.3& (SSQQ) as in bar 4 of Lara's Waltz of 1997.

In general, syncopated figures are carried out in less beats than the normal version: examples are the syncopated weave and quick open reverse turn.

7.   **Groupings of Figures**

Certain dancing figures follow naturally from one another and often appear in different sequences in the same order. Recognising these popular groupings is a great help in performing and remembering sequence waltzes.

Examples:-

Engagement and Denverdale Waltz	Back lock. Open impetus. Left whisk. Twist turn.
Waltz Cathrine	Whisk. Wing. Closed tele-mark. 123 natural turn.
Woodside Waltz	Whisk. Wing. Open tele-mark. Hover. Contra check. 123 natural turn.
Emmerdale Waltz	Whisk. Wing. Open tele-mark. Hover. Contra check. 123 natural turn.

CHAPTER 6

QUICKSTEPS AND SWINGS

The 'standard four' modern dances are the modern waltz, quickstep, slow foxtrot and modern tango. They are called 'modern' since they use the standard ballroom technique developed from 1924 onwards - ballroom hold and body contact are maintained at all times and great emphasis is placed on manner of performance.

Allied to these dances are old-time sequence dances performed at roughly the same tempo (apart from the Old-Time Waltz) which use in addition old-time dancing figures such as the twinkle, ronde, alemana and rotary turn.

Modern Dances	**Associated O/T Dances**
Modern Waltz (29-31 bpm)	Old-Time Waltz (40-44 bpm)
Quickstep	Swing
Slow Foxtrot	Saunter, Blues, etc.
Modern Tango	Old-Time Tango

A **Quickstep** is a foxtrot adapted to a faster tempo of 45-50 bpm. It is a happy, care-free sort of dance with its roots in the one-step (1914) and Charleston (1925). It is danced to lively martial music having 4 beats in the bar. Chassés of all types are common in quicksteps.

Swings are played at the same speed as quicksteps but to brighter (bouncy) music. They often contain a swing step in which one foot is moved to a low aerial position by swinging the leg. Although essentially old-time dances, few swings appeared before 1960.

MAYFAIR QUICKSTEP

The Mayfair Quickstep, arranged by Frank Short of Birmingham in 1956, has many old-time features and might well be called a swing. Ballroom hold is not maintained at all times - the dance starts and finishes in open hold and has solo turns for man and lady.

MAYFAIR QUICKSTEP   **DANCE SCRIPT**
BARS 1-8

Commence both facing LOD, inside hands joined. Man's steps described. Lady normal opposite unless stated otherwise. Tempo 48 bpm.

Bar		Count
1-4	**Walks - Point - Cross Chassé - Step and Point**	
1	Forward LF	S
	Forward RF	S
2	Forward LF down LOD	S
	Point RF DW (lady points LF)	S
3	Side RF to W releasing hold and passing behind partner	Q
	Close LF to RF	Q
	Side RF joining inside hands	S
4	LF fwd	S
	Point RF fwd releasing hold	S
5-8	**Open Turn to R (Lady: L) - Chassé Turn**	
5	RF fwd turning to R	S
	Side LF along LOD still turning	S
6	RF back still turning fcg DC agst LOD	S
	Point LF to side taking up ballroom hold	S
7	Side LF agst LOD turning R	Q
	Close RF to LF still turning	Q
	LF bk agst LOD	S
8	Side RF	Q
	Close LF to RF	Q
	Side RF agst LOD	S

1,2   *Walks, point*
Partners start in open hold - side by side with inside hands joined facing down LOD. Man takes 3 steps fwd L,R,L and points with his RF turning slightly toward his partner. Lady does the same on opposite feet pointing with her LF. Notice that weight is not transferred on the pointing step - both partners take 2 consecutive steps on the same foot, e.g. man's steps are point RF followed by side RF in bar 2.

3,4   *Cross chassé, step and point*
Releasing hands the man chassés sideways behind the lady towards the wall. The lady chassés sideways in front of him to the centre to change places. Both join inside hands, take a forward step and point.
The chassé (chasing step) is a basic movement in the quickstep. It consists essentially of 3 steps counted Quick, Quick, Slow with feet being closed on the second step. In bar 3 the steps are taken to the side (cross or side chassé).

5,6   *Open solo turn to R (lady to L), point*
Releasing hands both dancers make a half turn outwards taking 3 slow steps followed by a pointing step (also slow). They take up ballroom hold in promenade position facing DC agst LOD.

7,8   *Full chassé natural turn*
LF to side, close RF, LF back turning ⅜R. RF to side, close LF, RF to side turning ⅜R. Both chassés are timed QQS. (Chassé turns are similar to natural and reverse turns in the waltz with a timing of SQQ instead of SSS.)

Bar   Count

9-12   Outside Checks and Replace - Repeat Outside Check and Replace

9	LF fwd DW agst LOD (outside partner), L shoulder to L shoulder	S
	Replace weight to RF	S

10	Side LF along LOD	Q
	Close RF to LF	Q
	Side LF to face DW	S

11	RF fwd DW (outside partner), R shoulder to R shoulder	S
	Replace weight to LF	S

12	RF side against LOD	Q
	Close LF to RF	Q
	Side RF	S

13-16   Natural Chassé Turn Rotary - Step Point - Step Point

13	Side LF fcg agst LOD	Q
	Close RF to LF turning to R	Q
	LF back down LOD still turning	S

14	Side RF along LOD, toe pointing DC	Q
	Close LF to RF	Q
	Side RF still turning, to face LOD, opening out to starting position, inside hands joined, both facing LOD	S

15	Step LF along LOD	S
	Point RF fwd	S

16	Step RF along LOD	S
	Point LF fwd	S

9-12   *Outside check, chassé, outside check*
   The man steps outside the lady on her left side
   then replaces his weight to the back foot (the
   check). He then chassés to his left and checks on
   her right side. This movement is found in some
   cha cha cha figures (see page 185).

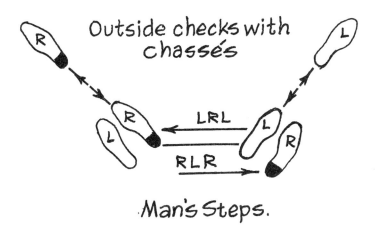

13,14   *Full chassé turn*
   A natural chassé turn as in bars 7,8. It is finished
   in promenade position and open hold is taken up
   again for the step points.

15,16   *Step points*
   Four slow steps:
   LF fwd, point RF, RF fwd, point LF.

Summary of the Mayfair Quickstep

Three forward walks. Point. Side chassé, changing places.
Step and point. Outward solo turns for man and lady.
Point. Natural chassé turn. Checks to L and R. Natural
chassé turn. 2 step points.

Popular version of Edith Farmer's dance of 1957

Ballroom hold. Man facing DW. Tempo: 44 bpm.

Bar   Count

1-4   Quarter Turn - Progressive Chassé - Check
1   Fwd LF DW; fwd RF turning ¼ R   SS
2   Side LF; close RF to LF; bk LF DC   QQS
3   Bk RF turning ¼ L; side LF   SQ
        Close RF to LF facing DW   Q
4   Fwd LF ptg dn LOD; RF fwd dn LOD   SS

5-8   Back Lock - Check - Point - Back Twinkle
5   Bk LF; bk RF agst LOD; lock LF over   SQQ
        front of RF (partner on right side)
6   Bk RF; bk LF (check), partner square   SS
7   Fwd RF down LOD; point LF in front   SS
        (Lady: point RF to rear)
8   Bk LF agst LOD; cls RF to LF; fwd LF   QQS

9-12   Check to Back Lock - Check - Fwd Lock
9   Fwd RF (check); bk LF agst LOD   SS
10   Bk RF; lock LF in front of RF; bk RF   QQS
11   Bk LF (check); fwd RF down LOD   SS
12   Fwd LF; lock RF bhd LF; fwd LF   QQS

13-16 Natural Spin Turn - Double Side Closes
13   Fwd RF tng to R to face W; side LF   SQQ
        down LOD; close RF to LF
14,15   Spin turn (or slow pivot) ¾ tn to R   SSSS
        in 4 steps LRLR ending square to
        partner
16   Side LF; close RF to LF and repeat   QQQQ
        both steps fcg DW

The above script differs from the original and ISTD scripts mainly in bars 4-6 - the checks and locks are taken along and against the LOD not to wall and centre.

BROADWAY QUICKSTEP   NOTES ON BARS 1-16

1-4   *Quarter turn, progressive chassé, check*
       Bars 1-3 are the full quarter turn figure (a zig-zag
       movement). A forward chassé quarter turn to R is
       followed by a backward chassé quarter turn to L
       (the progressive chassé). The last step of bar 4 is
       a RF fwd step which begins the check.

5-8   *Back lock, check, point, back twinkle*
       The check is completed by rocking back on to the
       LF; this is followed by the back lock which is a
       type of chassé with feet crossed instead of being
       parallel. Bar 7 is a RF fwd step followed by a LF
       fwd point (not a kick!). Bar 8 is a quick back
       twinkle which changes the leading foot preparing
       for the check which is to follow.

9-12   *Check, back lock, check, forward lock*
       Similar to bars 5-6. After the check the lock step
       is repeated in a fwd direction.

13-16 *Natural spin turn, double side closes*
       The same turn as in the waltz but carried out more
       rapidly and with a different timing - a 1-3 natural
       turn followed by a pivot and a spin step. Bar 16
       is 2 rapid side closes to L - 2 quick shuffles!

A good dance for practising checks and lock steps! The
weight needs to be kept well forward or backward in the
checks at the faster tempo.

Summary of the Broadway Quickstep (club version)

Forward chassé quarter turn to R. Backward chassé quarter
turn to L. Forward step and check to back lock. Check.
Point. Quick back twinkle. Check to back lock. Check to
forward lock. Natural spin turn. Two quick side closes.

Michael Davies and Betty Baker, Blackpool, 1984

*Ballroom hold. Commence facing DC. Man's steps
described. Lady dances normal counterpart unless stated
otherwise. Tempo: 48 bpm.*

Bar   Count

**1-4   Chassé Reverse Turn - Progressive Chassé -
         Forward Lock Step**
1   LF fwd DC comm turning L   S
         Side RF still turning   Q
         Close LF to RF backing LOD   Q
2   RF bk comm turning L   S
         Side LF still turning   Q
         Close RF to LF, facing DW   Q
3   Side LF and slightly fwd   S
         RF fwd in CBMP OP   S
4   LF fwd and slightly L   Q
         Cross RF behind LF   Q
         LF fwd and slightly L   S

**5-8   1 to 3 Natural Turn - Open Impetus Turn -
         Check in PP**
5   RF fwd in CBMP OP comm turning R   S
         Side LF still turning   Q
         Close RF to LF backing LOD   Q
6   LF back comm turning R   S
         Close RF to LF, heel turn, still   S
         turning (Lady: LF to side)
7   LF diag fwd, L shoulder leading   S
         (Lady: side RF along LOD in PP
         having brushed to LF)
         RF fwd in CBMP and PP, check   S
8   LF bk, small step in fallaway   Q
         Close RF to LF in PP   Q
         Side LF along LOD in CBMP and PP   S

1-4   *Chassé reverse turn, progressive chassé, forward lock step*
Bar 1 is the 123 waltz reverse turn with chassé timing SQQ.
The backward chassé turn of bar 2 is called a progressive chassé since it has the extra step LF to side and slightly L at the start of bar 3.
In bar 3 the LF side step and the RF forward step outside partner place the dancers in a comfortable position for the lock step of bar 4 - this is another chassé but with the feet crossed instead of being closed in parallel position.

Many modern sequence quicksteps and some swings start with a 1-3 chassé reverse turn and progressive chassé followed by a right foot step outside partner or a step in PP (Chandella Quickstep, Linden Swing).

5-8   *1-3 natural turn, open impetus turn, check in PP*
Bar 5 is the natural chassé turn preparing for the heel turn of the open impetus turn - the man moves his LF back and closes his RF to it while the lady moves her LF to the side. It is called an **open** impetus turn since the partners finish in PP.
In bars 7 and 8 the man checks forward in PP with his RF and recovers, something like a quick twinkle. Bar 8 finishes with a sideways step for the man preparing for the open natural turn which is to follow.

A **heel turn** as in bar 6 is a turn on the heel of the stepping foot. The closing foot is kept parallel throughout with a transfer of weight at the end of the turn.

Bar   Count

9-12   Open Natural Turn - Tipple Chassé to Right - Lock Step

9   RF fwd in CBMP and PP comm   S
       turning R (Lady: no turn)
       Side LF, still turning and bkg DC   Q
       RF bk with R shldr leading, bkg LOD   Q

10   LF bk in CBMP PO bkg DW and comm   S
       turning R
       Side RF pointing to LOD   Q
       Close LF to RF facing LOD   Q

11   Side RF and slightly fwd facing DW   S
       LF fwd and slightly L with L shldr ldg   Q
       Cross RF behind LF   Q

12   LF fwd and slightly L   S
       RF fwd in CBMP OP comm turning R   S
       and facing DW

13-16 Natural Zig-Zag - Natural Turn with Hesitation

13   Side LF and slightly back bkg DC   S
       RF bk in CBMP PO on L side and   S
       comm turning L

14   Side LF and slightly fwd ptg DW   S
       RF fwd in CBMP OP comm turning R   S

15   Side LF still turning   Q
       Close RF to LF bkg LOD   Q
       LF bk comm turn R   S

16   Side RF, heel pull, still turning   S
       Close LF to RF ww fcg DC   S

9-12   *Open natural turn, tipple chassé to right, lock step*
The open natural turn is started from PP and has chassé timing but the feet are not closed. The tipple chassé following can be seen as the progressive chassé of bar 2 taken to the right. Bars 9 and 10 are very similar to bars 1 and 2 taken in the opposite direction.

Bar 11 is the lock step. It seems to come very rapidly after the tipple chassé and the dancer needs to think ahead.

Bar 12 is the first part of the zig-zag and involves a ¼ turn to the right.

13-16   *Zig-zag, natural turn with hesitation*
Bar 13 and the first step of bar 14 complete the zig-zag (¼ turn R in bar 12 followed by ¼ turn L here). The remaining steps make up a natural chassé turn but the backward half of the turn occupies an extra beat giving a feeling of hesitation.

The following 16-bar sequence will start again with a chassé reverse turn to complete a figure which resembles the hesitation change in the waltz. (1-3 chassé natural turn with heel pull and hesitation in bars 15 and 16 followed by 1-3 chassé reverse turn in bar 1 of the next sequence.)

Summary of the Cameron Quickstep

1-3 chassé reverse turn. Progressive chassé (to L). 1-3 natural turn. Open impetus turn. Check in PP. Open natural turn. Tipple chassé (to R). Forward lock step. Natural zig-zag. Natural turn with hesitation.

SUMMARIES OF OTHER QUICKSTEPS

Universal Quickstep (1967)
Jacqueline Gipson (Forest Gate), 1st OBBD

Commence facing DW in normal hold. Tempo 48 bpm.

Bar

1-4	Walk. Nat turn. Back lock. Running finish.
5-8	Natural spin turn. V6.
9-12	Open finish. Fishtail. 1-3 natural turn.
13-16	Chassé R. Two locks. Chassé reverse turn.

V6 *(Back lock, back walks with ¼ turn to L)*
LF bk; RF bk; cross LF in front of RF;
RF bk; LF bk; RF bk (¼ turn L); LF to side.
The steps are timed SQQ, SSQQ.

Eivona Quickstep (1974)
Mrs. E. M. Crompton, Derby, 1st Blackpool

Start facing DC in ballroom hold. Tempo 48 bpm.

Bar

1-5	Progressive chassé R. Back lock step. Double tipple chassé.
6-8	Forward lock step. Hesitation turn.
9-12	Chassé reverse. Double progressive chassé.
13-16	Quick lock step. Check to compact chassé.

Quando Quickstep (1979)
Christine Hodgkinson, 1st NCDTA

Start in ballroom hold, man facing DC. Tempo 50 bpm.

Bar

1-4	Reverse lock. Progressive chassé. 2-5 forward lock.
5-8	123 natural turn. Back lock. Running finish.
9-12	Natural spin turn. Progressive chassé.
13-16	Fishtail. Natural spin turn with hesitation.

Kontiki Quickstep (1986)
Neil and Lesley Marshall, 1st SDTA

Ballroom hold facing DC. Tempo 50 bpm.

Bar
1-4   Progressive chassé R. Back lock. Running finish.
5-8   Forward lock. 123 natural turn. Chassé R.
9-12   Swivels. Telemark. Forward walk.
13-16   Double forward lock. Natural turn with hesitation.

Woodspring Quickstep (1988)
Ted and Sue Burroughs, 1st NATD

Ballroom hold, man facing DW. Tempo 48 bpm.

Bar
1-4   Walk. Open impetus to promenade. Wing.
5-8   Zig-zag. Reverse chassé. Progressive chassé.
9-12   Walk. Rock turn. 1-5 of V6.
13-16   6-8 of V6. Natural spin turn. 4-6 of reverse turn.

Chandella Quickstep (1990)
Philip Ainsley and Lorraine Heron, 1st UKAPTD

Ballroom hold, man facing DC. Tempo 48 bpm.

Bar
1-4   Chassé reverse. Check. Fishtail.
5-8   1-3 natural turn. Open impetus turn (lady wing).
9-12   Zig-zag. Closed telemark. Check.
13-16   Double lock. Natural turn. Change of direction.

Quality Quickstep (1992)
Ted and Sue Burroughs, 1st NATD

Ballroom hold, man facing DW. Tempo 48 bpm.

Bar
1-4   Walk. Half natural turn. Back contra check. Side chassé.
5-8   Side chassés. Walks. Zig-zag. Back lock.
9-12   Walk to running zig-zag. Back lock. 1-2 running finish.
13-16   3-4 running finish. Half natural turn. Back contra walks. 456 reverse turn.

SINDY SWING (1984)
Patricia Jay and Gary Fleetwood, 1st Minehead

The Sindy Swing (1984) is one of the most popular of recent award winners - a favourite with modern and old-time dancers alike. It has many features in common with the Mayfair Quickstep and is often used as an alternative to it for progressive dances.

SINDY SWING   DANCE SCRIPT BARS 1-8

Commence in open hold, partners facing down LOD, inside hands joined. Tempo 48 bpm.

Bar		Count
1-4	**Step Forward and Point - Step Back and Point - Forward Locks**	
1	LF fwd facing LOD; point RF fwd	SS
2	RF bk agst LOD; point LF bk	SS
3	LF fwd facing LOD	Q
	Cross RF behind LF facing LOD	Q
	LF fwd	S
4	RF fwd	Q
	Cross LF behind RF	Q
	RF fwd facing LOD, releasing hold	S
5-8	**Solo Turn - Chassé Square**	
5	LF fwd facing DC turning L	S
	(Lady: RF fwd turning R)	
	Side RF backing W	S
6	Side LF pointing to W	S
	Close RF to LF facing W and partner adopting double hold	S
7	LF fwd to W	S
	Side RF against LOD facing W	Q
	Close LF to RF facing W	Q
8	RF bk backing C	S
	Side LF backing C	Q
	Close RF to LF facing W and releasing hold	Q

94

1-4   *Step forward and point, step backward and point, forward locks*

The partners start side by side with inside hands joined (open hold) both facing down LOD. They step forward and point and then backward and point (on opposite feet).

Bars 3 and 4 are 2 forward locks - these are chassés with the feet crossed instead of the normal parallel foot closed position.

5-6   *Solo turn*

Both turn outwards (man to L, lady to R) travelling dn LOD and taking up double hold. (If the dance is progressive there is a change of partners here.)

7-8   *Chassé square (clockwise)*

This is like the clockwise waltz square in the Sweetheart Waltz with a different timing of SQQ,SQQ instead of all steps slow. This figure can be seen as 2 cross chassés - one forward, one backward. Double hold is released after the square.

Progressive Dances

The Mayfair Quickstep, Sindy Swing and Tango Serida are often performed in progressive fashion. After 16 bars there is a change of partners which takes place after the solo turns in the dances. Sometimes the MC may halt the sequence at some appropriate time to award small prizes to a selected couple. Quickstep music is usually used for the Mayfair Quickstep and Sindy Swing although samba, cha cha cha or two-step tracks may be used to give variety. The Tango Serida dances well to the rhythm and melodies of the Viennese Waltz.

Bar   Count

9-12   Outside Check - Chassé

Bar		Count
9	Side LF and slightly fwd facing DW joining RH to lady's RH (Lady: Side RF and slightly bk)	S
	RF fwd in CBMP OP facing DW, check	S
10	LF bk in CBMP backing DC agst LOD	S
	Side RF agst LOD facing W	Q
	Close LF to RF facing W and releasing hold	Q
11	Side RF and slightly fwd facing DW agst LOD joining LH to lady's LH	S
	LF fwd in CBMP OP facing DW agst LOD, check	S
12	RF bk in CBMP backing DC	S
	Side LF along LOD facing W	Q
	Close RF to LF facing W releasing hold	Q

13-16 Walks - Rotary Chassés - Side Closes

Bar		Count
13	Side LF and slightly fwd OP facing DW adopting double hold	S
	RF fwd in CBMP OP facing DW	S
14	Side LF along LOD backing DC adopting ballroom hold	Q
	Close RF to LF backing LOD	Q
	LF back	S
15	Side RF and slightly bk pointing DC	Q
	Close LF to RF facing DC	Q
	Side RF fcg LOD and releasing hold	S
16	Side LF and slightly fwd moving to C adopting open hold) (Lady: RF to side moving to W fcg LOD)	S
	Close RF to LF facing LOD	S

9-12   *Outside checks and chassé*
        The same steps as bars 9-12 of the Mayfair
        Quickstep but not in open hold and starting to the
        right of the lady (pages 84 and 85). In checking
        on the right hand side, right hands are joined - the
        check is then repeated to left of the lady (after the
        chassé) with left hands joined.

13-16   *Walks, rotary chassés, side closes*
        Ballroom hold is adopted for the walks and the
        rotary chassés; open hold for the side closes. The
        rotary chassés are the same as bars 7,8 and 13,14
        of the Mayfair Quickstep.

Summary of the Sindy Swing

Step forward and point. Step backward and point. 2
forward lock steps. Solo turns outwards. Clockwise chassé
square. Checks to L and R in single hold outside partner.
Walks. Rotary chassés. Side closes.

SUMMARIES OF SOME OTHER SWINGS

Linden Swing (1992)
Ken and Barbara Street, 1st ISTD

Normal ballroom hold, man facing, lady backing DC.
Lady counterpart. Tempo 48 bpm.

Bar

1-4   Chassé reverse turn.   Progressive chassé.
        Promenade lock.
5-8   Zig-zag. Outward turn. Chassé.
9-12   Check. Side and tap. Side and tap. Chassé.
13-16   Forward lock. Natural hesitation.

Singapore Swing (1992)

Theo and Doreen Ball, 1st IDTA

Commence in open hold, man facing DW, lady DC. Lady counterpart. Tempo 48 bpm.

Bar

1-4	Walk. Zig-zag. Fishtail.
5-8	Step and check. Chassé against LOD. Step and check. Chassé along LOD.
9-12	Step and swing left. Step and swing right. Chassé turn opening out to change of place in CPP.
13-16	Fishtail. Diagonal check. Double chassés to change of place.

Chicago Swing

Scripted from sight, about 1975

Partners face down line of dance with inside hands joined. Man's steps described. Time 4/4. Tempo 46/48 bpm.

Bar

1-4	Three forward walks with close. Two points to left side with close.
5-8	Two lock steps. Outward solo turns by man and lady. Take up double hold.
9-12	Step and point forward to wall. Step and point backward to centre. Steps and points repeated. (All steps and points danced with Charleston action.)
13-16	Side close and sway taken to left and to right. Take up original hold. Side step to left with drag close. Side step to right with drag close.

A popular dance in old-time circles.

CHAPTER 7

FOXTROTS

The modern slow foxtrot is the most typical of the dances in the 'English' (modern) style. It has long gliding casual steps and requires considerable space in the ballroom - it is a dance for good dancers. In contrast to the waltz the feet are seldom closed and figures like chassés are rare in sequence slow foxtrots.

Foxtrots are danced to music in 4/4 time with accents on the first and third beats. A common rhythm for one bar of music is:-

Slow	Quick	Quick
2 beats	1 beat	1 beat

The beats in the music are not stressed very strongly and the dancer must listen carefully to time his steps correctly.

The foxtrot is an offshoot of the one step and the rag arriving (in its early forms) from America in 1915. Opinions are divided as to whether it resembled the trotting steps of a fox or took its name from the stage routines of Harry Fox. Faster tempos were used and steps were often exaggerated when the music became lively. By 1925 the dance was beginning to separate into a slow foxtrot and a faster foxtrot-cum-Charleston which is now known as the quickstep.

Early sequence foxtrots closely resemble saunters having some waltz and tango figures and being danced to relaxed music in 4/4 time without too much accent on the beats. In the 1920's saunters provided a smooth restful alternative to the more vigorous dances with hopping and jumping steps which were the order of the day. The Melody Foxtrot has some elements of the saunter whereas the Glenroy Foxtrot is completely modern in style.

Start in normal ballroom hold with man facing, lady backing down LOD. Man's steps given, lady's are counterpart. Tempo 32 bpm.

Bar   Count

1-4   Points and Side Step to Left and Right
1   Point LF to L side; close LF to RF ww   QQ
       Point LF to L side; close LF to RF ww   QQ
2   Side LF to L; close RF to LF ww   SS
3   Point RF to R side ww; close RF to LF   QQ
       Point RF to R side ww; close RF to LF   QQ
4   Side RF to R; close LF to RF ww   SS

5-8   Walks - Chassés
5   LF fwd; RF fwd   SS
6   LF fwd (small step); close RF to LF   QQ
       LF fwd   S
7   RF fwd; LF fwd   SS
8   RF fwd (small step); close LF to RF   QQ
       RF fwd   S

9-12   Side Steps to Left and Right
9   Side LF (small step); close RF to LF   QQ
       Side LF (small step); close RF to LF   QQ
       (last 4 steps taken on ball of foot)
10   LF to side; close RF to LF ww   SS
11   Side RF (small step); close LF to RF   QQ
       Side RF (small step); close LF to RF   QQ
       (last 4 steps taken on ball of foot)
12   RF to side; close LF to RF ww   SS

13-16 Walks and Twinkles
13   LF fwd; RF fwd   SS
14   LF bk (small step); Close RF to LF   QQ
       LF fwd   S
15   RF fwd; LF fwd   SS
16   RF bk (small step); close LF to RF   QQ
       RF fwd; close LF to RF without weight   QQ

HARRY LIME FOXTROT   NOTES ON BARS 1-16

The Harry Lime Foxtrot created a sensation at the 1949 ISDC Festival in Blackpool when it was demonstrated by Henry Clarke and Mae Dickens.   Like many novelty dances it has its own music taken from the film 'The Third Man' with the unforgettable zither playing of Anton Karas.

The dance is really a saunter rather than a slow foxtrot - it has walks, chassés, points and twinkles.   It is a good teaching dance - easy to perform and remember since there is much repetition of figures (bars 5, 7, 13 and 15 are two forward walks; bars 3, 4, 7, 8, 11, 12, 15, 16 are repeats on the opposite foot of earlier bars).

Bars

1	Four consecutive steps on the LF - point to side, recover, steps repeated (QQQQ).
2	Side LF with weight; close RF to LF without weight (SS).
3,4	Bars 1 and 2 repeated on RF moving to R.
5	Two slow walks (LF, RF fwd).
6	Forward chassé (LRL).
7,8	Bars 5 and 6 repeated starting on the RF.
9	Side LF (small step); close RF to LF, steps repeated (QQQQ).
10	LF to side followed by a slow closing dragging step with RF without weight (SS).
11,12	Bars 9 and 10 repeated to the R.
13	Two slow walks (LF, RF fwd).
14	Quick back twinkle changing the leading foot followed by a LF fwd step (QQS).
15,16	Walks and twinkle of bars 13 and 14 repeated on the opposite foot. The final steps are RF fwd, close LF to RF ww (QQ) ready to begin the sequence again.

MELODY FOXTROT

There are at least two Melody Foxtrots. The script of the dance arranged by W. Hunter of Salford can be found in Bill Botham's Sequence Dances (North Star Publishers), 1953. The more popular version was said to have been arranged by two ladies from Birkenhead in 1956. Both are really saunters - squares, twinkles, lock steps are rarely found in slow foxtrots danced in modern style.

MELODY FOXTROT   DANCE SCRIPT BARS 1-8

Commence in normal hold, man facing LOD. The lady dances normal counterpart unless stated otherwise. Tempo 32 bpm.

Bar		Count
1-4	**Square - Step - Check - Twinkle - Lock**	
1	LF fwd down LOD	S
	Side RF to wall; close LF to RF	QQ
2	RF back	S
	Side LF to centre; close RF to LF	QQ
3	LF fwd down LOD	S
	RF fwd down LOD, check	S
4	Transfer weight back to LF	Q
	Close RF to LF	Q
	Forward LF; lock RF behind LF	QQ
5-8	**Square - Step - Check - Twinkle and Lock to Double Hold**	
5	LF fwd down LOD	S
	Side RF to wall; close LF to RF	QQ
6	RF back	S
	LF to side to C; close RF to LF	QQ
7	LF fwd down LOD	S
	RF fwd down LOD and check, preparing to step OP	S
8	Transfer weight back to LF	Q
	Close RF to LF; LF forward	QQ
	Lock RF behind LF OP in double hold	Q

1,2   *Clockwise square*
       Forward, side, close; backward, side, close - a
       clockwise square with chassé timing as in bars 7
       and 8 of the Sindy Swing.

3,4   *Step, check, twinkle, lock*
       In bars 3 and 4 after a LF fwd step, the RF is
       moved forward with a plié action (a flexing of the
       knees). Now follow 4 quick steps - weight is trans-
       ferred back to the LF and there is a rapid change
       of feet in what is known as a rear or back twinkle.

5-8   *Square, step, check, twinkle and lock to double
       hold*
       A repeat of bars 1-4 but changing to double hold
       for the last step.

It is said that the arrangers intended the whole dance to be
performed in ballroom hold but certainly double hold from
bars 9 to 12 seems more fitting.

Twinkles

Quick and slow twinkles are standard figures in social
rhythm dancing. They may be taken forward or backward
on either foot. They are used in marching to change the
leading foot to get into step. Leaving out a twinkle will
leave a dancer standing on the foot he needs to move with
- a hazard for beginners!

The man's steps for a RF forward twinkle are RF fwd; LF
closes to RF; RF bk. The timing is QQS for the quick
twinkle, SSS for the slow twinkle. The lady's steps are
the counterpart.

Bar   Count

9-12   Step - Check - Turning Twinkle to R - Walks - Check - Turning Twinkle to L

Bar		Count
9	LF forward	S
	RF forward, check, now facing DC	S
10	Replace weight to LF turning R	Q
	Side RF against LOD	Q
	LF fwd OP, L shoulder to L shoulder facing DW against LOD	S
11	RF forward DW	S
	LF fwd DW against LOD and check	S
12	Transfer wt back to RF turning L	Q
	Side LF along LOD	Q
	RF fwd down LOD, now facing LOD square to partner in double hold	S

13-16   Step - Check - Backward Three Step - Twinkle - Walks - Forward Closes

Bar		Count
13	LF forward down LOD	S
	RF forward down LOD, check	S
14	LF back	Q
	RF back	Q
	LF back	Q
	Close RF to LF	Q
15	LF forward down LOD	S
	RF forward down LOD	S
16	LF forward	Q
	Close RF to LF	Q
	Side LF to C	Q
	Close RF to LF	Q

9   *Forward walks*
        Two forward walks LF, RF down LOD in double
        hold preparing to check.

10   *Natural turning twinkle*
        LF bk turning R. Side RF agst LOD (some scripts
        have a closing step like a heel turn). LF fwd agst
        LOD taken outside partner (L shoulder to L
        shoulder). There is a ½ turn to R on these 3 steps.

11   *Forward walks*
        Two forward walks RF, LF against LOD preparing
        to check back.

12   *Reverse turning twinkle*
        The check back leads to a twinkle with a ½ tn L
        (bar 10 has a twinkle with ½ turn R). Many
        dancers take up ballroom hold here.

13   *Forward walks* - LF, RF fwd down LOD as bar 9.

14,15   *Backward three step, forward walks*
        Three quick steps LF, RF, LF taken against the
        LOD with a fourth quick step closing RF to LF.
        Bar 15 is LF, RF fwd down LOD.
        (Bars 15/16 include the backward twinkle.)

16   *Forward step and close, side step and close*
        LF fwd and close RF; LF to side, close RF.

Summary of the Melody Foxtrot

Clockwise square, walks, back twinkle and forward lock
repeated to end in double hold. Walks, turning twinkle
½ R. Walks, turning twinkle ½ L finishing square to
partner. Walks. Backward 3 step. Back twinkle. Walks.
Forward and side closes.

IRIS FOXTROT   DANCE SCRIPT BARS 1-8
Arranged by Terry Drogan, Droyslden, 1958

Commence in ballroom hold. Man fcg down LOD. Man's steps described. Lady dances normal counterpart unless stated otherwise. Tempo 31/32 bpm.

Bar		Count

1-4   Walks - Zig-zag - Walk to Check - Rocks into Promenade Position

Bar		Count
1	Forward LF	S
	Forward RF down LOD	S
2	Forward LF DC	Q
	Forward RF down LOD	Q
	LF behind RF	Q
	Forward RF down LOD	Q
3	Forward LF down LOD	S
	Forward RF (small step) and check	S
4	Back LF turning to R to face wall	Q
	Forward RF (small step) and square to wall	Q
	Rock back on to LF (rock turn)	S

5-8   Fallaway Chassé in PP - Prom Walks - Natural Pivot Turn - First Half Open Reverse Turn

Bar		Count
5	RF to side against LOD	Q
	Close LF to RF	Q
	Side RF against LOD	S
6	Forward LF in PP down LOD	S
	Forward RF turning to R	S
7	Forward LF across LOD	S
	Fwd RF turning to R, now facing diag to centre (⅝ turn to R on last 3 steps)	S
8	Forward LF, turning to L	Q
	Forward RF across LOD, still turning	Q
	Back LF still turning	S

106

1,2   *Walks, zig-zag*
       Two walks followed by a zig-zag which is a small
       turn to the L followed by a corresponding turn to
       the R; it finishes with RF fwd dn LOD (QQQQ).

3,4   *Walk, check, turning rocks into PP*
       Bar 3 is LF fwd, RF fwd (small step).
       Bar 4 is check back on LF turning ¼ R, rock
       forward on RF and back on LF towards wall.
       (Another version is to perform the rocks down
       LOD and make the turn at the start of bar 5.)

5   *Chassé against LOD in PP*
       Sideways chassé RLR (QQS) against LOD in PP
       preparing to move into a LF fwd step for the right
       turn which is to follow.

6-8   *Promenade walks, strong pivot turn to R*
       Bar 6 consists of a LF fwd step followed by RF
       fwd step starting to turn R (both in PP).
       Bar 7 is a strong turn completing the ⅝ turn to the
       R variously described as a natural pivot turn or
       promenade turn.
       This strong turn to the R is followed by a turn to
       the L, something like the hesitation change in the
       waltz although the feet are not closed at any stage.
       Bar 8 is the first half of this open foxtrot reverse
       turn to be completed in bar 9.

The Iris Foxtrot has some unusual features - chassés, steps
with feet closed and rock and pivot turns - figures which
rarely appear in modern slow foxtrots.

Bar   Count

**9-12 Second Half Open Reverse - Whisk - Feather
- Three Step**

9   Back RF, still turning to L   Q
       LF to side and slightly fwd ptg DW   Q
       Fwd RF on R side of partner   S

10   Forward LF to DW   Q
       Side and back RF, partners in PP   Q
       Place LF behind RF (whisk) in PP   S
       facing DC, down LOD

11   Forward RF, LF, RF outside partner   SQQ
       (Lady: turns to back LOD) (Feather)

12   Forward LF, RF, LF down LOD   SQQ
       (Lady: square to partner)

**13-16 Natural Pivot Turn - Whisk - Forward Closed
Change**

13   Forward RF, turning to R   S
       Side LF across LOD   Q
       Close RF to LF now backing LOD   Q

14   Back LF turning strongly to R to   S
       face down LOD
       Forward RF   S

15   Forward LF down LOD   Q
       Side RF   Q
       Place LF behind RF, now in PP   S
       facing diagonal to centre (whisk)

16   Forward RF to centre   Q
       Side LF to face LOD   Q
       Close RF to LF, now in orig position   S

9,10　*4-6 reverse turn, whisk*
Bar 9 is the backward half of the reverse turn finishing facing DW on the R side of the partner (R hip to R hip) - an open turn. (The original script has a closed reverse turn finishing with RF closing to LF.
Bar 10 is the back whisk - a common method if moving from square to promenade position.

11,12　*Feather, three step*
A three step (SQQ) moving outside partner followed by a three step (SQQ) square to partner.

13,14　*Natural pivot turn*
Bar 13 is the 1-3 of the natural turn (overturned) with timing SQQ. There is a ½ turn to R finishing backing down LOD.
Bar 14 completes the pivot turn. LF back pivoting strongly R followed by a RF fwd step down LOD (½ turn to R).

15,16　*Whisk, forward closed change*
Bar 15 is the whisk (similar to bar 10). Forward, side, cross behind, finishing facing centre.
Bar 16 is a RF forward closed change with a small turn to the R.

Summary of the Iris Foxtrot

Walks, zig-zag. Walk to check, rocks into PP. Fallaway chassé. Promenade walks. Natural pivot turn. Full open reverse turn. Whisk. Feather, 3 step. Natural pivot turn. Whisk. Forward closed change.

GLENROY FOXTROT   DANCE SCRIPT BARS 1-6
Tom Turner and Florence E. Smith, 1st ADA, 1976

Normal ballroom hold, man facing, lady backing DC.
Man's steps described, lady dances normal opposite
unless stated otherwise. Time 4/4. Tempo 30/32 bpm.

Bar   Count

1-4   Walk - Feather - Telemark - Curved Feather

1	LF fwd DC dn LOD; RF fwd DC dn LOD	SS
2	LF fwd DC dn LOD prepg to step OP	Q
	RF fwd DC dn LOD on R side partner	Q
	(R hip to R hip)	
	LF fwd DC dn LOD sq to ptnr, tng L	S
3	RF to side towards DC down LOD still	Q
	turning L (Lady: heel turn)	
	LF to side along LOD (toe pointing DW	Q
	down LOD)	
	RF fwd DW dn LOD on ptnr's R (R hip	S
	to R hip) comm curve clockwise to R	
4	LF fwd DW agst LOD still curving R	Q
	RF fwd agst LOD on partner's R	Q
	(R hip to R hip), check	
	LF bk dn LOD, ptnr on R turning R	S

5-6   Natural Impetus Turn - Feather Finish

5	Close RF to LF parallel position turning	Q
	to face DC down LOD	
	Still turning R, LF to side towards C,	Q
	backing DC agst LOD	
	RF back DC against LOD, turning L	S
6	LF to side and slightly fwd, toe pointing	Q
	DC down LOD	
	RF fwd DC down LOD on partner's R	Q
	(R hip to R hip)	
	LF fwd DC dn LOD square to partner,	S
	turning to L	

1,2   *Walk and feather*

A popular way of starting modern sequence slow foxtrots. After the initial slow LF step the feather begins with a RF forward step.   The next LF forward step is taken with a left shoulder lead to produce an opening-out movement for the following step taken outside the partner on her right side with CBMP - a most elegant movement. The final step brings partners into line.

3,4   *Reverse telemark, curved feather*

The telemark turn takes its name from a skiing turn originating in the Telemark district in Norway. It is a convenient way of turning through a comparatively large angle; it can be taken in both natural and reverse directions.

The man turns strongly to the left on the first two steps while the lady brings her feet together in a heel turn. He then walks somewhat against the line of dance outside the lady turning to his right (the curved feather). The last step of bar 4 is a check back still turning right - the first step of the impetus turn which is to follow.

5,6   *Natural impetus turn, feather finish*

The impetus turn is used in waltzes and quicksteps as well as slow foxtrots - it often follows steps 1-3 of a natural turn. RF is closed to LF in a heel turn followed by LF step taken to side and slightly back still turning R. The final step of bar 5 is RF back turning in opposite direction to left. Bar 6 is the feather finish where man steps outside his partner and then turns square again. This feather introduces the open telemark which follows in bar 7.

Bar   Count

7,8   Open Telemark - Natural Turn - Outside Swivel

7   RF to side towards DC dn LOD still   Q
        turning L (Lady: heel turn)
        LF to side towards DW down LOD in   Q
        promenade position
        RF fwd acr LF in promenade position   S
        moving towards wall, turning to R
        (Lady: no turn)
8   LF to side towards wall, slightly back   Q
        down LOD, square to partner
        RF back down LOD, R shoulder leading,   Q
        back DW down LOD
        LF bk DW down LOD, partner on R side   S
        (R hip to R hip), cross RF in front of LF ww,
        turning R to face DC down LOD in PP
        (Lady: outside swivel)

9-12   Roll Turn - Contra Check - Feather from Promenade Position

9   RF fwd towards DC down LOD in PP,   S
        turning R
        Side LF twds DC down LOD, sway to L   S
10   Turning R, correcting sway, replace weight   S
        to RF with body roll to face DW agst LOD
        LF fwd DW agst LOD, flexing knee,   S
        R shoulder leading, contra check
11   Replace weight to RF bk DC down LOD,   Q
        turning L to PP (Lady: no turn)
        LF to side along LOD in PP   Q
        RF fwd down LOD in PP   S
12   LF fwd DC down LOD turning partner L   Q
        and square
        RF fwd DC down LOD on partner's R   Q
        (R hip to R hip)
        LF fwd DC down LOD, turning L   S

7,8   *Open telemark, natural turn, outside swivel*
The open telemark is a telemark turn with the final steps taken in promenade position. As in bar 3 the man turns through a large angle to the left while the lady does a heel turn with feet together. The last step of bar 7 is the start of a natural open turn starting outside the lady in PP.

In bar 8 the man moves his LF to the side slightly back. He then takes two steps RF, LF backward leading his partner outside on his right. He then crosses his RF in front of his LF without weight (often called a loose lock) while the lady does her outside swivel. The outside swivel turns the lady from facing the man outside on her R (R hip to R hip) to promenade position. On the last slow step of bar 8 lady moves her RF forward outside partner and swivels on the ball of the foot making a half turn to the right; at the same time she closes her LF to her RF without weight in PP.

9-12   *Roll turn, contra check, feather from PP*
In bar 9 the man moves his RF forward from its loose crossed position turning right; this is followed by a LF side step swaying to the left.

The first step of bar 10 completes the roll turn - ½ turn to the right correcting the sway. The second step is the start of the contra check moving inwards to the partner with knee flexed and right shoulder leading.

Bar 11 completes the check and the partners move into PP.

Bar 12 is the feather preparing for the reverse wave which is to follow.

Bar   Count

13-16 Reverse Wave - Hover to Promenade Position - Chair - Slip Pivot

13	RF to side along LOD (Lady: heel turn), back DW down LOD	Q
	LF back DW down LOD	Q
	RF back DW down LOD comm turn L	S

14	LF to side towards DW down LOD	Q
	Replace weight to RF to side, hover action on last 2 steps	Q
	LF back DC down LOD. Partner on R side (R hip to R hip)	S

15	RF back DC down LOD, partner square turning L to PP (Lady: no turn)	Q
	Side LF along LOD in PP	Q
	RF fwd and across in PP down LOD, flexing knee, check, chair	S

16	Replace weight to LF back agst LOD, fallaway position, turn partner to L and square	Q
	Close RF to LF parallel position (Lady: slip pivot on last 2 steps)	Q
	Side LF towards C slight turn L, partner square	Q
	Close RF to LF parallel position facing DC down LOD in commencing position	Q

Summary of the Glenroy Foxtrot

Walks, feather. Reverse telemark, curved feather. Impetus turn with feather finish. Reverse open telemark. Open natural turn, outside swivel. Roll turn, contra check, feather from PP. Reverse wave. Hover to PP. Chair, slip pivot.

13,14   *234 reverse wave, hover to PP*

The last step of bar 12 and the steps of bar 13 are the first 4 steps of the 9 in the reverse wave. These 4 steps are really an open reverse foxtrot turn - similar to the waltz reverse turn without the feet being brought together at any stage; lady does a heel turn and the angle of turn is ½. The hover of bar 14 is a sideways rock from LF to RF rising on the toes and changing the weight with a hovering, floating action.

15,16   *Chair, slip pivot*

The man moves backwards and sideways in bar 15 turning the lady into PP. The man checks forward and with his RF across flexing his knee while the lady checks with her LF. This chair is a checking action in PP with inside legs.

In bar 16 the partners recover into fallaway position and the man moves the lady square by leading her into a slip pivot. The last two steps restore the original starting position - feet parallel, man facing DC. In the slip pivot the lady turns strongly to the left on the ball of her RF to face her partner. She then slips her foot between her partner's continuing to turn. There are really two pivots and a total turn of ¾. The slip pivot is the usual method of moving from the chair or fallaway to square position.

Comments

The Glenroy Foxtrot deserves careful study as it contains many of the common figures and amalgamations used in the more stylish modern foxtrots.

SUMMARIES OF OTHER FOXTROTS

Idaho Foxtrot (1959)
Bobby and Eileen Howe, Coventry, 1st IDMA

Ballroom hold, man facing LOD. Tempo 30/32 bpm.

Bars

1-4   Forward walks. Running zig-zag to forward lock.
        Point and closed finish.
5-8   Forward walks. Natural zig-zag to forward lock.
        Point and closed finish ending in PP.
9-12   Promenade walks. Solo telemark. Twinkle.
13-16   Counter promenade walks. Solo natural telemark.
        Rotary chassé.

Bermuda Foxtrot (1965)
Frank Short, Birmingham, 1st DTA (Mid)

Ballroom hold, man facing LOD. Tempo 30 bpm.

Bars

1-4   Forward walks and lock step.   Backward run.
        (Lady's solo reverse turn.)
5-8   Forward and backward walks.   Chassé (lady
        natural allemande).
9-16   Promenade turn. Four step to PP. Promenade
        turn. Four step to natural rotary chassé turn.

Karen Foxtrot (1982)
Derek and Irene Stevens, 1st Blackpool

Ballroom hold, man facing DW. Tempo 30 bpm.

Bars

1-4   Whisk. Feather ending. 1-6 reverse wave.
5-8   Open impetus. Chair. Same foot lunge. Lock
        steps, 2 and 3 feather.
9-12   1-4 reverse wave. Swivel. Curved feather. Hover
        impetus.
13-16   Hover cross from PP. Reverse turn.

Sefton Foxtrot (1969)
Arranged by ADA

Commence in ballroom hold, man facing LOD.

1-8   Walk. Feather. Wave. Weave. Three step. Open impetus turn. Chair.
9-16   Whisk. Feather. Closed telemark. Check. Feather to lunge. Link. Change of direction.

Raynette Foxtrot (1985)
Annette Sheridan and Ray Reeves, 1st Bognor Regis

Start in ballroom hold, man facing DC. Tempo 30 bpm.

1-4   Walk. Feather step. 1-4 reverse turn. Outside check.
5-8   Back feather. Feather finish. Three step opening to PP. Chair. Slip pivot.
9-12   Open telemark. Rotary hover cross from PP.
13-16 Underturned reverse turn. Check. Weave. Change direction. Back close.

Caribbean Foxtrot (1986)
Alwyn Leathley and Elsie Platts, 1st BCBD

Start facing DC in ballroom hold. Tempo 32 bpm.

1-4   Walks. Feather. Reverse turn. Hover corté.
5-8   Closed hover. Feather finish. Three step. Natural weave.
9-12   Whisk. Natural zig-zag from PP. Reverse wave.
13-16 Check to L and R. Feather finish. Change of direction.

Jayde Foxtrot (1987)
Derek and Irene Stevens, 1st Dance News, Slough

Ballroom hold. Man facing DC. Tempo 30 bpm.

1-4   Walk. Feather step. Whisk. Wing. Swivel L.
5-8   Curved feather. Open impetus tn. Weave from PP.
9-12   Change direction. Contra check. Slip pivot. Curved feather. Back feather.
13-16 Left side whisk. Untwist. Outside check. Back side close.

Ellis Foxtrot (1989)

Annette Sheridan and Ray Reeves, 1st NATD

Ballroom hold facing DC. Tempo 30 bpm.

1-4	Walk. Feather step. Open telemark. 1-5 natural weave.
5-8	6-7 natural weave. Whisk. Zig-zag. 1-3 wave.
9-12	4-6 wave. Open impetus turn. Chair. Contra check to PP.
13-16	Feather step from PP. Open telemark. Curved feather. Hesitation.

April Foxtrot (1992)

Graham and Avril Watkins, 1st Butlins, Bognor Regis

Ballroom hold, man facing DW. Tempo 30 bpm.

1-4	Hover to PP. Feather ending. Telemark turn. Feather OP.
5-8	Back feather. Feather finish. Drag hesitation. 3-6 weave.
9-12	Whisk. Zig-zag. Closed wing. Open telemark.
13-16	Double fallaway. Same foot lunge. Turning four step.

Tempro Foxtrot (1992)

Margaret Halliday, 1st NCDTA

Ballroom hold, man facing DW. Tempo 30 bpm.

1-4	Whisk. Feather from PP. Curving three step. Check to right.
5-8	Back feather. Feather finish. Zig-zag. 1-3 reverse wave.
9-12	4-6 reverse wave. Twinkle. Impetus turn. Feather finish. 1 of open telemark.
13-16	2-3 open telemark. 1-3 open natural turn from PP. Outside swivel. Weave from PP.

CHAPTER 8

TANGOS

Both modern and old-time tangos are danced to music in 2/4 time played in the tempo range of 30-34 bpm. For inventive sequence dance competitions the Official Board place them in the modern and old-time sections respectively. This gives tangos an advantage over the other dances since they can win prizes in two out of the three sections - this accounts to some extent for the preponderance of tangos among the new dances.

The differences between modern and old-time tangos are less marked than those between modern and old-time waltzes or between slow foxtrots and saunters. Dance leaders do not always announce whether a particular tango is modern or old-time and many sequence dancers of average ability dance them in exactly the same way - considerable technical skill is required to reveal the modern tango in its full glory.

Old-time tangos have a long history - the Square Tango (1920) and Royal Empress Tango (1922) are still popular in the clubs. They have much in common with saunters and share several of the same dancing figures - some tangos dance well to saunter music and vice versa. Various holds are used and solo turns and alemanas are permitted.

The modern tango as a ballroom dance dates from about 1935 - it has a special type of ballroom hold with the lady held more to the right and a set of standard figures. The approved hold is maintained at all times and there are exaggerated quick movements of the head and other members of the body.

THE SQUARE TANGO (1920)

This dance is sometimes attributed to Mr. John E. Evans - he was at one time Secretary of the Empire Society and operated a script service in Wales in the 1940's.

THE SQUARE TANGO   **DANCE SCRIPT**
                                        BARS 1-12

Commence in ballroom hold, man facing, lady backing down line of dance. Man's steps given, lady dances counterpart. Tempo 32 bpm.

Bar   Count

1-8   Clockwise Square - Side Steps with Drag Closes
         - Figures Repeated
1   LF fwd   S
         RF to side   Q
         Close LF to RF   Q
2   RF bk   S
         LF to side   Q
         Close RF to LF   Q
3   LF to side (long step)   S
         RF closed to LF with a dragging   S
         action without transfer of weight
4   RF to side (long step)   S
         LF closed to RF without weight   S
5-8   Bars 1-4 repeated

9-12   Walks - Three Steps
9   Forward LF, RF   SS
10   Forward LF, RF, LF   QQS
11   Forward RF, LF, RF   SQQ

(The 8 steps in bars 9-11 are more easily remembered as SSQQ, SSQQ)

12   LF fwd starting to turn R   S
         RF fwd turning ¼ R to face wall   S

Bar   Count

13-16 Turn and Check - Rock Turn

13	Side LF and back (short step)	S
	RF bk to C (check)	S
14	LF fwd turning R	S
	Side RF to R still turning R	S
15	Side LF to L still turning R	S
	Side RF to R still turning R	S
16	Side LF to L still turning	S
	RF bk agst LOD (check)	S

This dance is fairly straightforward since it involves considerable repetition and for the most part the man is facing and the lady backing down LOD.

The rock turn of bars 14-16 is easier to perform than describe! The RF is kept well forward under the partner for the turns. During the rocks the RF is turned to the right without much lateral movement while the LF moves to the side. The total turn on the 5 steps is ¾ - from man facing W to man facing down LOD. The last step is a rock back on to the RF to be followed by a small LF fwd step beginning the next sequence.

Summary of the Square Tango

Clockwise square. Drag closes to L and R. Clockwise square. Drag closes to L and R. Eight steps down LOD (SSQQ, SSQQ). Forward pivot to wall, rock back to centre. Five slow rocking steps with RF forward turning R to finish facing LOD. Rock back on to RF.

TANGO SERIDA   DANCE SCRIPT BARS 1-8
Arranged by Rita Pover, 1st Dance News, 1961

Partners commence facing LOD. In shadow hold - man's R shoulder behind lady's L shoulder with RH round her waist, LHs joined (see page 39). Both start with LF and dance identical steps for bars 1-3, thereafter man's steps described, lady dances normal counterpart unless otherwise stated. Tempo 32 bpm.

Bar   Count

1-4   **Forward and Backward Walks - Forward and Backward Chassés (Lady: Solo Turn to R)**

Bar	Step	Count
1	LF fwd down LOD	S
	RF fwd bending knee slightly	S
2	LF back against LOD	S
	RF back bending knee slightly	S
3	LF fwd; close RF to LF	QQ
	LF fwd bending knee slightly, L shoulder leading	S
4	RF diag bk agst LOD releasing hold whilst lady turns to R	Q
	Close LF to RF fcg DW	Q
	RF to side against LOD taking up ballroom hold in PP	S
(4	Lady: Side RF agst LOD starting to turn R; close LF to RF now fcg DW agst LOD	QQ
	RF fwd agst LOD, still turning	Q
	Close LF to RF tng to face DC in PP	Q)

Both now dance on opposite feet.

5-8   **Promenade Link - Lunge - Backward Chassé - Side Chassé to PP**

Bar	Step	Count
5	Side LF in PP along LOD	S
	RF fwd and across in PP and closing LF to RF ww turning partner square so that she is backing DW	QQ
6	LF fwd DW R shoulder leading	S
	RF fwd slightly bending knee, R shoulder leading	S

7	LF back twds C, L shoulder leading	Q
	Almost close RF to LF	Q
	LF back, brush RF to LF without weight, turning partner into PP	S
8	Side RF agst LOD in PP	Q
	Close LF to RF in PP	Q
	Side RF agst LOD in PP	S

TANGO SERIDA   NOTES ON BARS 1-8

1,2   *Forward and backward walks*

Man and lady dance side by side in shadow hold taking the same steps ('on the same leg') - LF, RF forward (check); LF, RF bk. As the RF moves forward the knees bend slightly (a plié).

3,4   *Forward and backward chassés*

Man and lady chassé LRL forward releasing hold. The man chassés RLR backwards while the lady performs a solo turn to the right; they take up ballroom hold in PP facing DW. (The lady takes 4 steps to the man's 3 to get on opposite feet.)

5,6   *Promenade link, lunge*

Bar 5 is the promenade link - a common method of moving from PP to ballroom hold. On the second step the man turns strongly left and then closes LF to RF without weight turning lady square and backing DW.

Bar 6 is the lunge - a very elegant figure. The man takes two slow steps LF, RF with right shoulder leading; knees are bent slightly on second step; direction is DW.

7,8   *Backward chassé, side chassé to PP*

Bar 7 is a backward chassé (LRL) recovering from the lunge of the previous bar; partners turn into PP on last step. Bar 8 is a side chassé in PP (RLR) taken against LOD.

Bar   Count

9-12 Promenade Walks - Outward Solo Telemark Turns by Man and Lady - Promenade Link - Contra Check

9   Side LF along LOD in PP   S

       RF fwd and across releasing hold   S

10   LF fwd down LOD, turning to L   QQ
       (Lady: turns to R); side RF still tng,
       now back to back with partner

       Side LF along LOD continuing to turn,   Q
       now facing DW

       Close RF to LF resuming hold in PP   Q

11   LF to side along LOD in PP   S

       RF fwd and across   Q

       Close LF to RF ww tng to face W   Q

12   LF fwd towards W, knee slightly bent   S
       turning partner square to back W

       RF back   S

13-16 Backward and Forward Chassés - Hesitation (Lady: Natural Solo Turn) - Two Side Closes

13   LF back; close RF to LF; back LF   QQS
       On last step make a slight body turn to L,
       stretching body upwards, feet left apart
       in open position

14   Transfer wt fwd to RF; close LF to RF   QQ

       Fwd RF DW; close LF to RF ww, turning   QQ
       lady into PP, releasing hold

15   Man pauses with feet together, transfer   QQ
       wt to LF, placing hand on hip and holding
       RH out twds ptnr who is making solo turn
       away from him

       RF fwd twds partner, bending knee slightly,   S
       take partner's LH in RH
       (Lady: makes just over 1 complete turn to
       her R giving her LH to her partner and
       swinging her R arm gently outwards towards
       the wall
       (Both now dance on the same feet)

16   Replace wt to LF; close RF to LF   QQ
          Small step to side with LF, turning   QQ
          slightly L to face LOD; close RF to LF,
          now in starting position
          (Lady: LF to side towards partner;
          close RF to LF; long step LF to side
          towards partner; close RF to LF)

TANGO SERIDA   NOTES ON BARS 9-16

9,10   *Promenade walks, outward solo turns*
        After two walks in PP, the hold is released and the
        man and lady both turn outward in quick solo turns
        - QQQQ.

11,12   *Promenade link, contra check*
        In bar 11 (like bar 5) the man moves from PP to
        square finishing with feet together (weight on RF)
        facing DW.
        The contra check of bar 12 is like the lunge in bar
        6 without the extra forward step.

13,14   *Backward and forward chassés*
        Bar 13 is a backward chassé similar to bar 7.
        Bar 14 is a forward chassé finishing in PP and
        preparing to release hold.

15,16   *Hesitation, two side closes*
        In bar 15 the man hesitates and moves his RF
        forward whilst the lady makes a solo turn to the R.
        Bar 16 is two side closes.
        If the dance is to be progressive both the lady's
        turn in bar 15 and the side closes in bar 16 are
        taken down LOD.

Summary of the Tango Serida

See page 126.

TANGO LAS VEGAS   DANCE SCRIPT BARS 1-8
David Bullen, 1st ADA, 1978

Commence in normal ballroom hold with man facing, lady backing LOD. Man's steps described.   Lady counterpart unless stated.   Tempo 32 bpm.

Bar   Count

1-4   Walks - Zig-zag - Walks - Turn to Back LOD
1	LF fwd down LOD	S
	RF fwd down LOD	S
2	LF fwd down LOD, comm to turn L	Q
	RF to side along LOD	Q
	LF bk DW agst LOD, comm turn R	Q
	RF to side fcg LOD with lady on L	Q
3	LF fwd down LOD (L hip to L hip)	S
	RF fwd down LOD OP	S
4	LF fwd down LOD OP comm to turn R	Q
	Pivoting to R, close RF to LF now bkg LOD	Q
	LF side to wall	Q
	Close RF to LF	Q

5-8   Walks (Lunge) - Twinkle - Closed Wing for Lady - Four Step to PP
5	LF fwd agst LOD	S
	RF fwd agst LOD relaxing knee	S
6	LF back down LOD	Q
	Close RF to LF moving lady to R side	Q
	LF fwd agst LOD OP (R hip to R hip)	S
7	RF fwd agst LOD OP	Q
	LF side to wall (small step)	Q
	RF back agst LOD now with lady on L side	S
	(L hip to L hip)	
	(Lady: LF bk agst LOD; RF side to wall	
	passing across man; LF fwd down LOD OP)	
8	LF fwd agst LOD OP turning to L	Q
	Close RF to LF still turning	Q
	LF to side along LOD in PP	Q
	Close RF to LF facing LOD in PP	Q

This tango splits up neatly into 4 sections, each starting with 2 forward walks. Bar 1 and bar 5 have 2 walks square to partner; bars 9 and 13 have 2 walks in PP. (See also forward walks in bars 3 and 11.)

1-4   *Forward walks, reverse zig-zag, forward walks to left, turn to back LOD*

The forward steps of bar 1 are followed by the zig-zag in bar 2 which is ⅛ turn to L followed by ⅛ turn to R.

Bar 3 is 2 walking steps outside the lady on her left (L hip to L hip).

Bar 4 starts with a third step outside the lady starting to turn R. The turn is completed by a pivoting step finishing backing down LOD with lady square. The bar is completed by a side step and close.

5-7   *Walks, twinkle, closed wing*

Bar 5 is 2 forward walks relaxing the knees on the second - sometimes called a lunge.

Bar 6 starts with a backward twinkle (back, close and forward) moving lady to the R side. The next 2 steps are LF fwd and RF fwd outside partner on R (R hip to R hip).

Bar 7 continues with the closed wing. After a small LF step to side, the man takes a step backward with his RF against the LOD moving the lady from his left-hand to his right-hand side.

8   *Four step to PP*

Bar 8 is a turning four step - this is a normal four step with a turn to the left finishing in PP.

Bar   Count

9-12 Walks - Solo Turn - Walks - Brush - Tap - Whisk - Tap

9	LF fwd down LOD in PP	S
	RF fwd down LOD in PP	S
10	Releasing hold, LF fwd turning to L (Lady: R)	Q
	RF to side along LOD still turning	Q
	LF side along LOD	Q
	Close RF to LF to face LOD in PP, taking up ballroom hold	Q
11	LF fwd down LOD in PP	S
	RF fwd down LOD in PP	Q
	Close LF to RF ww turning inwards to face partner	Q
12	LF to side to C ww (Lady: RF side to wall ww)	Q
	Whisk LF behind RF	Q
	RF fwd down LOD in PP	Q
	Tap LF down LOD in PP	Q

13-16 Walks - Promenade Turn - Chair - Slip Pivot

13	LF fwd down LOD in PP	S
	RF fwd down LOD in PP	S
14	Turning to R, LF to side and across LOD	Q
	RF to side still turning	Q
	LF fwd down LOD	Q
	Close RF to LF in PP facing LOD	Q
15	LF fwd down LOD in PP	S
	RF fwd down LOD in PP relaxing knee (chair)	S
16	LF back agst LOD (fallaway position) (Lady: RF back agst LOD)	Q
	RF back agst LOD turning lady square (Lady: LF fwd agst LOD - slip pivot)	Q
	LF side to C	Q
	Close RF to LF to starting position	Q

9,10   *Walks, solo turn*

After the 2 forward walks in PP of bar 9 the hold is released.   Both partners perform outward solo turns (man to L, lady to R) taking up ballroom hold and finishing with feet together in PP facing down LOD.

11,12   *Walks, brush, tap, whisk, tap*

Two walks in PP down LOD are followed by LF closing without weight to RF (the brush) turning inwards to partner (SQQ).

Still keeping the weight on the RF the man turns outwards and taps with his LF to the side then crosses the LF behind the RF in the whisk.   The final steps are RF fwd and LF tap in PP facing down LOD (QQQQ).

13,14   *Walks, promenade turn*

Bar 13 is 2 walks, LF, RF fwd in PP.

Bar 14 starts the promenade turn with LF to side and across LOD turning R (Lady: RF fwd between man's feet).

The strong turn to R continues with RF to side and LF fwd down LOD.   The bar ends with RF closing to LF in PP facing LOD.

15,16   *Chair, slip pivot*

Bar 15 is LF fwd, RF fwd relaxing the knees (Lady: RF to side, LF fwd).   This is a movement where both check inside together called a chair (SS).   In bar 16 the weight is transferred back to the LF in fallaway position starting to turn the lady to the left.   The next step is RF back against LOD turning lady square (the slip pivot).   The last 2 steps are LF to side to centre, close RF to LF.

SUMMARIES OF OLD-TIME TANGOS

Tango Las Vegas (1978) (O/T)
David Bullen, 1st ADA

Tango hold, man facing down LOD. Tempo 32 bpm.

Bars

1-4	Forward walks. Zig-zag. Walks to left of lady. Turn to back LOD.
4-8	Walks (lunge). Twinkle. Closed wing for lady. Four step to PP.
9-12	Walks. Outwards solo turns. Walks. Brush, tap. Whisk, tap.
13-16	Walks. Promenade turn. Chair. Slip pivot.

Tango Serida (1961) (O/T)
Rita Pover, 1st Dance News

Start in shadow hold facing down LOD.

Bars

1-4	LF forward, RF forward (with plié). Repeated backwards. Chassé LRL forward releasing hold. Chassé RLR back (Lady: solo turn R) taking up ballroom hold in PP. *(Bars 1-3 on same leg.)*
5-8	Promenade link turning square. Lunge (LF, RF fwd, DW). Chassé LRL back; chassé RLR to side.
9-12	Promenade walks. Outward solo turns finishing in PP. Promenade link (as bar 5). Contra check.
13-16	Chassé LRL back. Chassé RLR forward in PP. Hesitate (Lady: solo turn R). Two side closes LRLR.

Royal Empress (1922) (O/T)
Adela Roscoe, 1st Blackpool

Commence in tango hold, man facing down LOD.
Tempo 32 bpm.

Bars

1-4   Two steps forward and plié, 2 steps backward and plié. Diagonal chassés to L and R finishing in PP.
5-8   Two steps to centre, chassé forward LRL, swivel inwards to R. Repeat last 2 bars to wall in CPP.
9-12   Two steps along LOD, promenade pivot turn finishing in PP facing down LOD. Two steps along LOD and point, pivot inwardly to face against LOD.
13-16   Repeat last 2 bars against LOD. Two rotary chassés (full turn to R).

Trelawney Tango (1954) (O/T)
Stanley Ross, Watford, 1st BATD

Commence in tango hold, man facing down LOD.
Tempo 32 bpm.

Bars

1-4   Walks. Reverse turn to outside check. Outside walks. Forward and side closes.
5-8   Repeat bars 1-4. Commence RF turning right and ending in PP.
9-12   Slow turn and point. Four quick change. Oversway.
13-16   Promenade closes. Open reverse turn. Check. Lady's solo turn to closed finish.

Tango Solair (1970) (O/T)
C. W. Stewart, Northampton, 1st OBBD

Ballroom hold. Man facing down LOD. Tempo 32 bpm.

Bars

1-8	Walks. Progressive link. Outside swivel to turning closed finish. Reverse turn. Repeated against LOD finishing in PP.
9-16	Solo reverse and natural turns. Zig-zag. Contra check. Promenade walks. Same foot lunge. Promenade chassé. Closed finish.

Tango Manhatten (1989) (O/T)
Philip Ainsley and Lorraine Heron, 1st Blackpool

Ballroom hold, man facing LOD. Tempo 32 bpm.

Bars

1-4	Walks. Outside check. Outside check. Turning rock.
5-8	Repeat bars 1-4 but facing against LOD, end facing DC.
9-12	Open reverse turn. Closed finish. Same foot lunge. Step point.
13-16	Fallaway. Step lock step. Step point (Lady: alemana). Side close.

Tango Leanne (1992) (O/T)
Philip Ainsley and Lorraine Heron, 1st UKAPTD

Ballroom hold, man facing down LOD. Tempo 32 bpm.

Bars

1-4	Walks. Zig-zag. Turning four step. Solo pivot turn. Side close.
5-8	Repeated against LOD. End bar 8 man ends facing, lady backing DC.
9-12	1-6 reverse turn (Lady: outside). Progressive link. Syncopated locks.
13-16	Walks. Travelling solo turn. Chair. Slip pivot. Side close.

SUMMARIES OF MODERN TANGOS

Modern tangos have the following characteristics:-

(a)   the ballroom hold used is more compact with the lady further to the right;

(b)   the partners stand obliquely to the line of dance with the man's right hip and shoulder forward - this makes the walks curve slightly to the left;

(c)   the knees are flexed more than in the other modern dances and steps are taken at the last moment with a crisp staccato action;

(d)   there is no rise or fall or body sway;

(e)   there are exaggerated quick movements of the head and other members of the body.

Tango Suhali (1970) (Mod)
Joan Wilson, Heanor, 1st IDTA

Tango hold facing DW. Tempo 32 bpm.

1-4	Two walks. Progressive link. Fallaway promenade to outside swivel.
5-8	Two steps promenade link. Type of four step to end on partner's L side. Two strong side walks. Switch to contra check.
9-12	LF rock. Back lock to tap. Contra walk forward outside partner. Contra walk back, PO. Syncopated turn to end in PP.
13-16	Promenade to L whisk. Fallaway twist turn. Promenade link.

Lancaster Tango (1987) (Mod)
Annette Sheridan and Ray Reeves, 1st IDTA

Ballroom hold facing LOD. Tempo 33 bpm.

1-4	Two walks. Open telemark. Double fallaway.
5-8	Same foot lunge. Turning five step. Closed promenade.
9-12	Two walks. Open telemark to drop oversway. Chassé to whisk.
13-16	Swivels to outside swivel. Promenade link. Closed promenade.

Tracy Tango (1987) (Mod)
Sylvester Burrows, 1st BATD

Tango hold facing DW. Tempo 32 bpm.

Bars

1-4　Walks. Basic reverse turn. Four step.
5-8　Whisk. Syncopated lock in PP right point line. R chassé to fallaway position.
9-12　Outside swivel. Promenade link. Turning four step. Promenade turn. Rock turn.
13-16　4-7 of rock turn. Open telemark. RF lunge.

Torque Tango (1991) (Mod)
Albert and Florence Clark, 1st NCDTA

Tango hold facing DW. Tempo 33 bpm.

Bars

1-4　Walks. Progressive link. Chassé. Chassé to whisk.
5-8　Link. Closed promenade. Open reverse. Open finish.
9-12　Outside swivel. 2.3 promenade link. Four step. X line. Back twinkle. Forward close.
13-16　Side point to promenade tap. Walk. Syncopated lock. Closed promenade.

Telecon Tango (1992) (Mod)
Alwyn Leathley, 1st ADA

Ballroom hold facing LOD. Tempo 34 bpm.

Bars

1-4　Walks. Basic reverse turn to open finish. Swivel and tap.
5-8　Fallaway promenade. Natural promenade. Rocks.
9-12　Closed finish. Link. Syncopated lock and tap.
13-16　Left whisk. Fallaway twist turn and tap. Slip pivot. Side close.

CHAPTER 9

TRADITIONAL OLD-TIME DANCES

Old-time waltzes, gavottes, two-steps, schottisches, polkas, minuets and mazurkas were popular in the 19th century. Sequence forms of these dances came back into fashion after the second world war and still continue to win awards at inventive sequence dance competitions.

Unlike modern dances and saunters, blues and swings the feet are often at an angle of about 90° instead of being parallel; there are 5 standard positions derived from classical ballet. Steps are taken more on the toes and springing and hopping steps are more common. The dances are arranged from a relatively small pool of figures which often have French names.

The three main traditional old-time dances which win awards in modern inventive sequence dance competitions are:-

1.   O/T Waltzes - 3/4 time, tempo 40-44 bpm. The old-time waltz has long been known as 'the queen of the ballroom' - the majority of early sequence dances contain old-time waltz elements.

2.   Two Steps - 6/8 time, tempo 44-56 bpm. Energetic dances performed to marching tunes. Most contain the *pas de basque* figure and finish with bars of waltzing.

3.   Gavottes - 4/4 time, tempo 23-25 bpm. The oldest and slowest of the sequence dances. The basic step is the *pas de gavotte* which consists of: step, close, step, aerial (foot raised to ankle height).

Various Old-Time Figures

(a)   *Pas de valse* - step; step; close to 3rd position with weight. This is the forward closed change of the modern sequence waltz in a different guise - it is a straight line figure (rather than triangular) and finishes with the feet at an angle. In the same way it is used to change from a natural to a reverse turn and vice versa.

He If the partners are in ballroom hold the lady will do a backward *pas de valse* while the man does the forward figure. If in side-by-side position (open or shadow holds), they will usually do the same *pas de valse* with opposite feet.

(b)   *Pas glissade* (gliding step) - step; close to 3rd position **with weight**. Often found as a side close with the feet at an angle.

(c)   *Pas glissé* (another gliding step) - step; close to 3rd position **without weight**. The closing foot is now free to move in some other direction.

(d)   *Balancé* - step; close to 3rd position **without weight**. This differs from the *pas glissé* in having a rocking, swaying action - a rise to the ball of the foot on the first step is followed by a lowering at the end of the second step.

(e)   *Pas de basque* - A LF *pas de basque* to side consists of - spring to side with LF; close RF to LF with transfer of weight releasing LF slightly from floor; replace weight to LF pointing toe of RF downwards.

He The figure can be made simpler (and less attractive) by replacing the spring with a step.

The Five Positions of the Feet

All the positions may have one or both feet with the toe, ball of foot or heel on the ground.

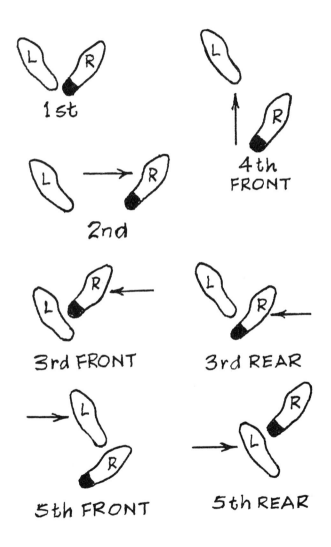

1st

2nd

4th FRONT

3rd FRONT

3rd REAR

5th FRONT

5th REAR

LILAC WALTZ   DANCE SCRIPT BARS 1-12
Alfred Halford, 1st OBBD, 1951

Partners side-by-side with man facing DW, lady facing DC. Man's RH holds lady's LH, man's LH placed on hip, thumb to rear. Tempo 44 bpm.

Bar		Count
1-4	**Zephyrs - Back Lock Steps**	
1	LF fwd down LOD	1
	Swing RF fwd to low aerial position	2 3
2	Cross RF loosely in front of RF	1
	Raise RF to low aerial position	2 3
3	RF back agst LOD	1
	Cross LF in front of RF	2 3
4	RF back agst LOD	1
	Cross LF in front of RF ww	2 3
5-8	**Solo Turns to Left and Right**	
5	LF fwd down LOD starting to turn L releasing hands	1 2
	RF to side along LOD still turning L	3
6	LF bk down LOD still turning to face DW agst LOD joining LH to lady's RH	1 2
	Rise on ball of LF leaving RF extended	3
7,8	Repeat bars 5 and 6 against the LOD starting with the RF and turning R	
9-12	**Points - Balancés**	
9	LF fwd down LOD, point RF fwd	123
10	RF fwd down LOD, point LF fwd	123
11	LF back to C facing partner	1
	Close RF to LF without weight (balancé away from partner)	2 3
12	RF fwd to wall and partner	1
	Close LF to RF without weight (balancé towards partner)	2 3

The dance should have a definite rising and falling movement except on bars 9 and 10 where there is a body rise only.

1-4   *Zephyrs and back lock steps*

Bar 1 consists of a LF fwd step by the man followed by the zephyr - this is a swinging of the R leg from the hip across and in front of the L leg at calf height.

In bar 2 the RF is touched lightly to the floor and the R leg swung forward and backward across the L leg with another zephyr action.

Bar 3 is a slow backward lock step crossing LF in front of the RF.

Bar 4 is the same as bar 3 but the LF crosses without weight. (The lady's steps in bars 1-4 are the same but on opposite feet.)

5-8   *Solo turns to left and right*

Bar 5 is LF fwd, RF to side turning L and releasing hands (lady turns to R).

In bar 6 the man moves his LF back down the LOD to finish the turn facing DW agst LOD with RF extended; he hesitates for the last 2 beats holding the lady's R hand in his L hand.

Bars 7 and 8 are repeats of bars 5 and 6 but starting with the R foot and turning R.

9-12   *Points and balancés*

Bar 9 is LF fwd, point RF and hesitate.

Bar 10 is RF fwd, point LF and hesitate.

Bar 11 is the back balancé - LF back to centre closing RF back to it without weight with a rocking, swaying action; hands are released but remain in the air.

Bar 12 is the forward balancé - same as bar 11 but moving towards partner.

Partners now take up waltz hold.

(In the balancés the feet are closed in 3rd position.)

Bar   Count

13-16 Natural Waltz Turns

Man dances 3 bars of waltz turns followed by *pas de valse*; lady dances 4 bars of waltz turns. This is to achieve the original starting side-by-side hold.

LILAC WALTZ   NOTES ON BARS 13-16

The complete old-time waltz turn for the man consists of a rearward **rotary** half turn and a forward progressive half turn. The lady dances the progressive half turn while the man performs the rotary half turn and vice versa.

Natural Rotary Half Turn (Man's steps)	Turn	Timing
1. LF to side, sltly bk, turning R	⅛R	S
2. RF closes to LF in 5th position rear	⅛R	S
3. Rising on toes with weight on LF, pivot to the right finishing with RF in 5th position front	¼R	S

Natural Progressive Half Turn (Man's steps)	Turn	Timing
1. RF fwd between partner's feet, turning R	⅛R	S
2. LF to side still turning R	⅛R	S
3. RF closes to LF in 5th position front	¼R	S

Summary of the Lilac Waltz

Step and swing RF across LF. Swing back. Backward lock step. Backward lock step without weight. Solo turns to L and R. 2 step points. Balancés away from and towards partner. 4 bars of waltzing.

FYLDE WALTZ — DANCE SCRIPT BARS 1-16

Tom Arnold (1902)

Side-by-side position, man facing DW, lady facing DC.
Man's RH holds lady's LH. Tempo 40 bpm.

Bar		Count

1-8   Pas de Valse - Balancé Fwd - Pas Glissade - Half Waltz Turn - all repeated agst LOD

Bar	Description	Count
1	LF fwd; RF fwd; close LF to RF	123
2	RF fwd rising on toe; close LF slowly to RF ww (balancé forward)	123
3	Glide LF back agst LOD; close RF slowly to LF (rearward glissade)	123
4	Inward rotary half natural turn to face DW agst LOD changing holds	123
5-8	Bars 1-4 repeated starting with RF agst LOD and finishing facing DW	

9-16   Progressive Half Reverse Turn - Pas Glissade - Rotary Half Reverse Turn - Pas Glissade - Waltz Turns

Bar	Description	Count
9	LF fwd into a progressive half reverse turn releasing hands and finishing DC agst LOD	123
10	Glide RF bk along LOD taking lady's RH in LH, still fcg DC agst LOD; close LF slowly to RF	123
11	RF bk into rotary half reverse turn joining hands in double hold to finish fcg W	123
12	Glide LF to side along LOD turning slightly to face DW agst LOD; close RF slowly to LF taking up waltz hold	123
13-16	Man dances 3 bars of natural waltz turns with a pas de valse, lady dances 4 bars of natural waltz turns	

Summary of the Fylde Waltz

Open position - Pas de valse and balancé forward. Pas glissade to rear. Inward half waltz turn to face opposite direction. All figures repeated agst LOD. Outward half waltz turn along LOD, pas glissade. Inward half waltz turn, pas glissade. Waltz 4 bars.

PRIDE OF ERIN WALTZ

C. S. Wood, 1st prize BATD, 1911

Commence in double hold with hands joined at shoulder level, with man facing W, lady facing C. Man starts with LF, lady with RF. Tempo 48 bpm.

Bar   Count

1-8   Promenade Walks - Chassés - Repeat Agst LOD

1	LF to side along LOD (fcg DW)	123
2	Cross RF over LF	123
3	Chassé to L (LRL)	123
4	Point RF to R agst LOD, LH raised above shoulder	123

5-8	Bars 1-4 repeated agst LOD to end pointing LF to L down LOD

9-16   Crosses and Points - Solo Waltz Out - Solo Waltz In

9	Cross LF over RF agst LOD	123
10	Point RF to R	123
	(On bars 9 and 10 raise LH, lower RH)	
11	Cross RF over LF down LOD	123
12	Point LF to L raising RH and fcg LOD	123

13,14	Man releases lady's RH retaining her LH and waltzes outward (end back to back, man taking lady's RH in his LH and drawing his LF to his RF)	123 123
15,16	Repeat bars 13 and 14 coming back to original position	

Bars 1, 2, 4 (and several others) have 1 step to 3 beats (1 bar) of music - this makes for a longer sequence (32 bars instead of 16).

Bar   Count

**17-24 Balancé to Partner and Change of Places -
Repeat and Back to Own Place**

17	Rejoining hands LF fwd to W on L side of partner	1
	Close RF to LF	2 3
18	RF back; close LF to RF	123
19,20	Waltz to each other's places, lady turning under man's L arm, man's RH on his hip (allemande)	123 123
21-24	Bars 17-20 repeated returning to original places (change of places and return)	

**25-32 Chassé along LOD with Inside Point Chassé
Against LOD - Inside Point**

25	Chassé L (LRL) with hands extended	123
26	Swing RF across LF and point in low aerial position	123
27	Chassé R (RLR) with hands extended	123
28	Swing LF across RF and point in low aerial position	123
29-32	Two complete natural waltz turns opening out to original starting position	

NOTES ON THE PRIDE OF ERIN WALTZ

Bars 3 and 7 - The chassés are step, close, step with a timing of 1.2.3. (Modern chassés in the quickstep are timed QQS.)

Bars 13 and 14 - Many dancers replace the waltz turn by a *pas de valse* (step, step, close with weight) followed by a forward balancé.

Although there are relatively few dancing figures in old-time waltzes there are many movements of arms, feet and head which require tuition and considerable practice to achieve a high standard.

THE EVA THREE STEP

The Eva Three Step was arranged by Sydney W. Painter of Manchester in 1903 and named after his daughter. As originally written it was a stately dance performed to music in 4/4 time at gavotte tempo (23-25 bpm). It is called a three step since there are 3 steps and point in all the first 4 bars. As originally danced it had allemandes with the lady in bower position and was somewhat difficult to describe. It has remained popular over the years but undergone considerable changes to become a pleasing party dance - sometimes performed with stamping of feet. Recommended music on one script is 'The Teddy Bears' Picnic'! It is an 8-bar sequence danced to music in 4/4 time at 32-34 bpm.

THE EVA THREE STEP	DANCE SCRIPT
	BARS 1-4

Man's steps.   Start in open position.   Tempo 32 bpm.

Bar		Count

1-4   Three Step and Point - Three Step and Point Passing Partner - Three Step and Point Diagonally Forward - Three Step and Point Return to Place

Bar		Count
1	LF fwd; RF fwd; LF fwd	123
	Turn sltly R, point RF twds wall	4
2	RF diag fwd, preparing to pass lady on her L, join LHs	1
	LF fwd passing partner	2
	RF fwd tng L, rel LHs, place LH on hip	3
	Point LF fwd, now fcg DC	4
3	LH on hip, no hold, LF diag fwd	1
	RF fwd, look twd partner	2
	LF fwd, still looking, turning sltly R	3
	Point RF fwd twds wall	4
4	Tng sltly L to face LOD, RF bk	1
	LF bk; RF bk turning sltly R	2 3
	Point LF twds wall taking lady's LH in RH - now back in starting position	4

Bar   Count

5-8   **Solo Waltz Outward - Swing Steps**
        - Waltz Finalé

5   Solo waltz, making one complete turn   1&2
           to L to end facing partner
           Join both hands, raise arms shoulder high   3&4

6   LF to side; swing RF in front of LF and to   1.2
           L, foot raised from floor, toe pointing down
           RF to side; swing LF in front of RF and to   3.4
           R, foot raised, toe pointing down

7,8   Taking waltz hold, dance 2 complete waltz   1&2
           natural turns, opening out at finish to   3&4
           original starting position

THE EVA THREE STEP (Popular Version)

Movements of the head and arms are simplified and the
solo turns and swings of bars 5 and 6 are replaced by
steps and swivels. The timing is 1234 in bars 1-6; 1&2
3&4 in bars 7 and 8.

*Start in side-by-side position facing down LOD with man's
RH holding lady's LH.*

Bar

1-4   **Three Step and Points**
           Three steps and a point (sometimes with a body
           turn on pointing step) taken as follows:-

1   Forward LF, RF, LF, pointing RF
2   Behind lady to R, RF, LF, RF, point LF
3   In front of lady to L (to Centre)
4   Backwards to regain original position

5-8   **Steps and Swivels - Waltz Turns**
           Turn inwards taking up double hold

5   3 steps DW swivelling to face DC
6   3 steps DC swivelling to face DW
7,8   Taking up waltz hold, dance 2 natural waltz turns
           opening out to original starting position

Old Time Sequence Dancing

This chapter on traditional dances is rather brief since sequences in this style rarely win prizes in recent inventive dance competitions. Of 270 winners from 1990 to 1995 there were only 9 gavottes, 6 old-time waltzes and 2 two-steps. There is also a cultural bias against these dances in some areas - they are not taught or danced.

Nevertheless some dancers prefer to attend sessions wholly devoted to the old-time style - they enjoy the music of the past and the order and formality of earlier years. The inclusion of progressive dances and set dances for four couples tend to mix people together and promote a friendly atmosphere at these gatherings.

The interests of old-time dancers are well served by the 'Society for the Preservation and Appreciation of Old-Time Music and Dancing' (The Old Time Society) which publishes a newsletter giving news of current events, dance club reports and a dance diary. (Secretary: Fred Boast, 8 Bourne Way, Addlestone, Surrey, KT15 2BT.)

Two very useful books for old-time dancers are:-

(a) 'A Guide to the Theory and Technique of Sequence Old-Time Dancing', British Council of Dancing (1997). (Available from Hearn and Spencer - ref. 9, page 46.)

(b) 'Sequence Dancing' by Michael Gwynne, A. & C. Black, London (1989). (30 pages of old-time theory and 45 detailed scripts of older dances.)

A recent video is:-

'Introduction to Old Time Dancing - A beginner's guide'. 10 Old Time dances demonstrated by Ted and Sue Burroughs. (Savoy Music, P. O. Box 271, Purley, Surrey, CR8 4YL, 0181 660 5046.)

CHAPTER 10

SAUNTERS AND BLUES

Saunters and blues are danced to music in 4/4 time in the foxtrot tempo range of 29-31 bpm; for saunters stress is placed on the 1st and 3rd beats, for blues all beats have some accent.

Saunters and foxtrots have a common origin and some early foxtrots should really be called saunters. The saunters of today are based on slow leisurely walking steps with some old-time and foxtrot figures. Saunters are well-suited to more mature dancers and only waltzes (and some old-time tangos) are more popular in the clubs.

Many efforts have been made to promote the blues as a go-as-you-please ballroom dance. Alex Moore (dancing with his sister) won the Blues Competition at Princes Galleries in 1923. Early editions of his 'Sequence Dancing' (1936) give details of the forward and backward walks and various chassés and turns. (These are omitted from the 9th edition of 1980.) The blues walk has a characteristic lilting movement obtained by relaxing the supporting knee followed by a slight rise on the ball of the foot. The slow social rhythm dance described in ballroom manuals is a form of blues without rise or fall. Some early sequence blues like the Georgella and Manhattan Blues are danced at quickstep tempo.

Several other old-time sequence dances have affinities with saunters. Strolls start in side-by-side position and have many steps danced 'on the same foot'; parades are similar but played in quickstep tempo. Sways have sway figures, glides have gliding steps as in skating. There are twinkles, jinks, rags, strutters and various party dances.

147

Arranged by Harry Boyle in 1919

Start in normal ballroom hold, man facing, lady backing down LOD. Man's steps described, lady's steps counterpart. Time 4/4. Tempo 28 bpm.

Bar   Count

1-4   Forward Walks - Rocks
1   LF fwd (Lady: RF bk)   S
        RF fwd   S
2   LF fwd   S
        RF fwd   S
3   Without moving feet, rock back to LF   S
        Rock fwd on RF   S
4   Rock back on LF   S
        Rock fwd on RF   S

5-8   Forward Walks - Rock and Swivel
5   LF fwd   S
        RF fwd   S
6   LF fwd   S
        RF fwd   S
7   Rock back on LF   S
        Rock fwd on RF   S
8   Rock back on LF   S
        Rock fwd on RF swivelling slightly   S
        to R to face DW

9-12   Scissors Steps
9   LF diag fwd DW over and across RF   S
        Point RF to side, toe to floor towards W   S
10   Swivelling L on both feet, move RF diag   S
        to L over and across LF
        Point LF to side, toe to floor towards C   S
11,12   Repeat bars 9 and 10

Bar   Count

13-16 Chassés Left and Right - Rotary Chassé - Natural Turn

13	LF diag fwd (Lady: RF diag bk)	Q
	Close RF to LF	Q
	LF diag fwd	S
14	RF diag fwd (Lady: LF diag bk)	Q
	Close LF to RF	Q
	RF diag fwd	S
15	LF to side turning R	Q
	Close RF to LF still turning	Q
	LF back still turning R, now backing LOD	S
16	RF to side still turning	Q
	Close RF to LF still turning	Q
	RF fwd to finish facing LOD	S

Summary of the Yearning Saunter - Bars 1-16

Bar

Start in waltz hold facing down LOD

1,2	4 steps fwd	SSSS
3,4	Rock back and fwd twice	SSSS
5,6	Repeat 4 steps fwd (bars 1,2)	SSSS
7,8	Repeat rocks (bars 3,4) swivelling slightly to R to face DW on last step (Lady: backing DW)	SSSS
9	LF across RF, point RF outside partner	SS
10	Swivel to L on both feet, RF across LF, point LF outside partner	SS
11,12	Repeat scissors steps of bars 9,10	SSSS
13	Diagonal chassé, LF, RF, LF to L	QQS
14	Diagonal chassé, RF, LF, RF to R	QQS
15,16	Rotary chassé turns (2 x ½ turns to R) (step, close, step, step, close, step)	QQS QQS

SAUNTER TOGETHER

Arranged by Bob and Winn Oliver, Butlins, 1975

Ballroom hold, man facing, lady backing down LOD.
Man's steps given, lady dances counterpart unless
otherwise stated. Time 4/4. Tempo 28 bpm.

Bar   Count

1-4   **Walks - Zig-zag - Outside Checks - Close**

Bar	Step	Count
1	LF fwd; RF fwd	SS
2	LF fwd comm to turn L	Q
	RF to side	Q
	LF bk DW on R side partner	Q
	(R hip to R hip) comm turn R	
	RF to side, square to partner	Q
3	LF fwd DC on L side partner, check	S
	RF bk turning to L	Q
	LF to side	Q
4	RF fwd DC agst LOD on R side partner	S
	Check back on LF turning to L	Q
	Close RF to LF facing agst LOD	Q

5-8   **Walks agst LOD - Zig-zag - Checks**
            - Close in PP

Bar	Step	Count
5-7	Repeat bars 1,2,3 moving agst LOD	
8	RF fwd DW on R side partner, check	S
	LF bk	Q
	Close RF to LF in PP (Lady: Turns ¼	Q
	to R on last 2 steps to end in PP)	

9,10   **Promenade Walks to Fallaway**

Bar	Step	Count
9	LF to side in PP along LOD	S
	RF fwd in PP comm to turn R into	S
	fallaway (Lady: RF to side in PP; LF fwd	
	in CBMP and PP comm to turn R)	
10	LF to side and slightly bk still turning R	Q
	RF bk still turning, now bkg DW	Q
	LF bk down LOD in fallaway leaving RF	S
	extended (Lady: RF fwd down LOD still tng;	
	LF to side and slightly bk now bkg DC; RF	
	bk dn LOD in fallaway leaving LF extended)	

The first 10 bars are performed in ballroom hold. The early part of the dance is split into 4 bar sections by walks:-

Bar 1	2 walks down LOD
Bar 5	2 walks against LOD
Bar 9	2 walks in PP down LOD

1-4 *Walks, zig-zag, outside checks*
After 2 walks down LOD in bar 1 there is part of a natural zig-zag which consists of a ⅜ turn to the left followed by a turn to the right.

Bars 3 and 4 are checks to either side of partner with a side step in between.

LF check on L side; recover; side step RF check on R side; recover; closing step with partner square.

These turning steps are much easier to perform if the body is swung in the direction of the turn.

5-8 *Walks agst LOD, zig-zag, checks, close in promenade position*
Steps in bars 1-4 repeated against the line of dance but finishing in PP (lady turns ¼ to R on last step of bar 8).

9-10 *Promenade walks to fallaway*
Bar 9 consists of 2 walks, starting to turn into fallaway position. The man completes an open ½ turn to the right which moves the partners from PP down LOD to PP against LOD.

Finally both take a step back (man LF, lady RF) into fallaway position leaving the inside foot extended - bodies inclined away from one another.

Bar   Count

11-12 RF Whisk - Twist Turn

11	RF fwd agst LOD comm to turn R	Q
	LF to side still turning	Q
	RF crosses behind LF bkg DW agst LOD	S
	(now in double hold)	
12	Comm to twist to R allowing feet to	QQQQ
	uncross and end fcg W in double hold	
	(Lady: Takes 4 curving steps round man	
	to R, RF,LF,RF closing LF to RF fcg C	QQQQ)

13-16 Chassé Sways (Lady turning to shadow hold)
- Step, Point - Natural Turn to Closed Finish

13	LF to side along LOD	Q
	RF closes to LF	Q
	LF to side along LOD with sway to L	S
	leaving RF extended	
14	RF to side agst LOD releasing hold	Q
	LF closes to RF	Q
	RF to side agst LOD with sway to R	S
	now in DW position with LF extended	
	adopting shadow hold	
	(Lady: Comm to turn L, LF fwd agst LOD;	
	RF closes to LF without weight still turning;	
	RF to side agst LOD now fcg wall in	
	shadow position with LF extended)	
15	LF to side along LOD	S
	(lady dances same as man)	
	Point RF fwd DW	S
	(lady dances same as man)	
16	RF fwd DW	Q
	LF closes to RF without weight	Q
	adopting ballroom hold	
	LF to side to C turning to face LOD	Q
	RF closes to LF	Q
	(Lady: RF fwd DW comm to turn R;	
	LF to side along LOD, small step fcg W;	
	RF to side to C; LF closes to RF)	

11,12 *RF whisk, twist turn*

Both partners start in fallaway position and take a forward step turning inwards to face one another and taking up double hold (man facing, lady backing C). The man completes the left whisk by crossing his RF behind his LF.

In bar 12 the man is turned by the lady to the R untwisting his feet (the twist turn) - she takes 4 quick curving steps. The result is a change of places with man fcg, lady bkg W in double hold.

13,14 *Chassé sways to left and right*

Bar 13 is a sway to the L with partners facing one another in double hold.

Bar 14 is a sway to the R with the lady turning to L into shadow position on the last step (both partners are now side by side, LH holding LH and RH holding RH at shoulder height).

15,16 *Step point, lady's solo turn, closed finish*

In bar 15 the man and lady both move LF to side along LOD pointing RF fwd DW.

In bar 16 the man turns the lady into ballroom hold finishing with a side close.

Summary of the Saunter Together

1-8 Two walks down LOD, zig-zag. Checks to L and R finishing square to partner. Figures repeated against the LOD finishing in PP.

9-16 Walks to fallaway. Twist turn. Lady unwinds man taking up double hold. Chassé sway to L. Chassé sway to R turning to shadow hold. Step, point on same feet. Lady turns R into ballroom hold. Closed finish.

Moonlight Saunter (1919)
C. J. Daniels

Ballroom hold. Man facing, lady backing down LOD. Tempo 28 bpm.

Bars

1-4	(and 5-8)	Walks. Outside swivels.
9-12	(and 13-16)	Walks. Check. Square.
17-20	(and 21-24)	Promenade turns. Points.
25-28	(and 29-32)	Walks. Balancé. Promenade turn.

The bars in brackets are sometimes omitted to give a 16-bar sequence.

Britannia Saunter (1958)
Official Board of Ballroom Dancing

Ballroom hold. Man facing, lady backing down LOD. Tempo 28 bpm.

Bars

1-4   Walks. Open twinkle.
5-8   Promenade walks. Reverse telemark. Promenade walks.
9-12   Point. Natural turn. Rock. Reverse quarter turn.
13-16   Walk. Chassé. Pivot turn. Twinkles.

Sherrie Saunter (1949)
Nancy Clarke, 1st IDMA (Rhyl)

Ballroom hold. Man facing, lady backing LOD. Tempo 34-36 bpm.

Bars

1-4   Walks. Twinkles.
5-8   Walks and fallaway turns.
9-12   Quarter turns to right and left.
13-16   Quick zig-zags.

Saunter Revé (1961)
Rita Pover, 1st OBBD (Filey)

Ballroom hold. Man facing, lady backing down LOD.

Bars

1-4	Walks. Lilt. Promenade chassés.
5-8	Pliés and diagonal locks to wall and centre.
9-12	Lady's solo turn. Sways and chassés. Promenade turn and chassés.

Kingfisher Saunter (1990)
Graham and Kathy Thomson, 1st Blackpool

Normal ballroom hold. Man facing, lady backing LOD.

Bars

1-4	Walks. Zig-zag. Same foot lunge. Turning four step to shadow hold.
5-8	Walks. Zig-zag. Sway to R. Turning four step. (Bars 5-7 man and lady same steps.)
9-12	Promenade walks. Natural fallaway. Left whisk. Change places to shadow hold.
13-16	Walks. Solo turn. Sway to L. Chassé. Side close.

Redrose Saunter (1991)
Steven and Diane Shaw, 1st Butlins Pwllheli

Ballroom hold. Man facing, lady backing LOD. Lady normal counterpart. Tempo 28 bpm.

Bars

1-4	Walks. Zig-zag. Lock step. Swivel. Lock step.
5-8	Walks. Zig-zag. Lock step. Swivel. Lock step to PP.
9-12	Walks to natural fallaway. Solo outward turn. Step point.
13-16	Fallaway. Lock step and sway. Side close. (Lady underarm turn L.)

LINGERING BLUES DANCE SCRIPT BARS 1-16
Arranged by Adela Roscoe in 1929

Ballroom hold, man facing, lady backing down LOD. Man's steps described, lady dances counterpart unless stated. Time 4/4. Tempo 32 bpm.

Bar   Count

1-4 Rocks and Three Steps

1	LF fwd (short step)	Q
	Rock back on RF	Q
	LF fwd	S
2	RF fwd (short step)	Q
	Rock back on LF	Q
	RF fwd	S
3	LF, RF, LF fwd	QQS
4	RF, LF, RF fwd finishing in PP	QQS

5-8 Promenade Rocks and Three Steps
Bars 1-4 repeated in promenade position. The lady swivels to the L taking up ballroom hold with man facing, lady backing down LOD.

9-12 Quick Closed Twinkles and Steps

9	LF fwd; close RF to LF	QQ
	LF bk; close RF to LF	QQ
10	LF fwd; RF fwd	SS
11,12	Repeat bars 9 and 10	

13-16 Side Close Figures

13	LF to side (to C); close RF to LF ww	QQ
	RF to side (to W); close LF to RF ww	QQ
14	LF to side; close RF to LF **with weight**	QQ
	LF to side; close RF to LF ww	QQ
15	RF to side (to W); close LF to RF ww	QQ
	LF to side (to C); close RF to LF ww	QQ
16	RF to side (to W); close LF to RF **with weight**	QQ
	RF to side (to W); close LF to RF ww	QQ

1-8   *Rocks, three steps*
        In bars 1-4 there are 2 rocks and 6 forward
        steps (QQS,QQS) taken with a running
        action in ballroom hold. These figures are
        repeated in PP in bars 5-8.

9-12   *Quick closed twinkles, steps*
        Bar 9 is a quick closed twinkle (a twinkle
        with a 4th closing step).
        Bar 10 is 2 forward walks.
        These figures are repeated in bars 11, 12.

        Bars 9 and 11 are sometimes performed
        with a zig-zag action:-

LF fwd, turn L to face DC	Q
RF to side DW	Q
LF bk turn R to face LOD	Q
Close RF to LF	Q

13-16   *Side close figures*

13	Rock brushes to L and R	QQQQ
14	Step and close to L	QQ
	Rock brush to L	QQ
15	Rock brushes to R and L	QQQQ
16	Step and close to R	QQ
	Rock brush to R	QQ

        (Bars 15, 16 are bars 13, 14 on
        opposite feet.)

        A simpler variation is to replace the rock
        brushes of bars 13 and 15 by sways (S
        instead of QQ) taking 3 quick steps in bars
        14 and 16:-

13	Sway to L on LF	S
	Sway to R on RF	S
14	Three quick steps LRL diag to C	QQS
15,16	Bars 13, 14 repeated on	SS
	opposite feet	QQS

BALMORAL BLUES   DANCE SCRIPT BARS 1-10
Arranged by Robert Stewart in 1971

Commence in double hold, man facing DW, lady facing DC. Man's steps described, lady dances counterpart unless stated. Tempo 30/32 bpm.

Bar		Count
1-8	**Chassé - Promenade Zig-Zag - Fwd Lock - Outward Turn to Fwd Lock - Repeated**	
1	LF to side along LOD; close RF to LF	QQ
	LF to side along LOD	S
2	RF fwd and across in CBMP	Q
	LF to side along LOD turning sltly R	Q
	RF bk and across in CBMP turning L	Q
	LF to side along LOD	Q
3	RF fwd dn LOD releasing hold of lady's RH	Q
	Cross LF behind RF	Q
	RF fwd down LOD releasing hold and making ½ turn to L to face agst LOD	S
4	Extend LF agst LOD taking lady's R hand in man's L hand	Q
	Cross RF behind LF	Q
	LF fwd DW agst LOD swivelling ⅛ to L on LF	Q
	Close RF to LF ww adopting double hold and fcg DW agst LOD	Q
5-8	Bars 1-4 repeated agst LOD starting with RF	
9-10	**Changes of Place (Lady's Allemandes)**	
9	LF fwd DW, man taking lady's RH in LH and turning L	Q
	RF to side and slightly bk still turning (Lady: RF fwd crossing in front of man turning R under man's raised LH)	Q
	LF bk DW agst LOD with RF extended	S
10	RF fwd DC turning R	Q
	LF to side and slightly bk still turning (Lady: allemande in front of man)	Q
	RF bk DC agst LOD, LF extended	S

1,2   *Chassé, promenade zig-zag*
Partners face inwards to one another (something like PP) in double hold (opposite hands joined).
Bar 1 is a chassé in PP down LOD. The **alignments** are man facing DW, lady facing DC; the **direction** of movement is down LOD.
Bar 2 is a turn first to R then to L with less turn and body movement than the normal zig-zag.

3-8   *Forward lock, outward turn to lock*
Bar 3 is a forward lock step LF crossing behind RF (lady opposite). Both partners take a step forward, release hold and make a half solo turn outwards swivelling on both feet - a figure often found in saunters and other old-time dances.
Bar 4 is another forward lock step (man's RF crosses behind LF) finishing with man brushing RF to LF. The partners are now in their original position but facing this time against LOD.

Bars 5-8 are bars 1-4 repeated against the LOD starting with the RF.

9,10   *Two changes of place, lady's allemandes*
In bar 9 man moves L,R,L sideways turning the lady in front of him to the R under his raised LH (allemande).
In bar 10 the man moves sideways back to his original position R,L,R turning lady to her L under his raised L hand.
Partners take up double hold.

(Changes of place are sometimes referred to as 'cross overs'.)

Bar   Count

11-12 Sways to L and R - Chassé to Shadow Hold
11	LF to side along LOD with slight turn	S
	to R sway to L in double hold	
	Replace weight to RF swaying to R	S
12	LF to side along LOD	Q
	Close RF to LF starting to turn L	Q
	releasing hold with RH	
	LF fwd DW still turning	Q
	Close RF to LF taking up shadow hold	Q
	(side-by-side, LH's joined, man's R	
	arm round lady's waist); both face DW	
	preparing to move fwd on same foot	

**13-16 Diagonal Runs to R and L - Walk - Check
- Back Lock**
13	LF fwd DW	Q
	RF fwd DW	Q
	LF fwd swivelling ¼ to L	Q
	Close RF to LF ww (brush step)	Q
14	RF fwd DC	Q
	LF fwd DC	Q
	RF fwd swivelling ¼ to R	Q
	Close LF to RF ww (brush step)	Q

(Man's and lady's steps same in bars 13,14)

15	LF fwd DW releasing hold	S
	RF fwd DW on R side of partner	S
	adopting double hold	
	(Lady: LF fwd DW tng L; RF to side	
	and slightly bk still tng; LF bk DW	QQS)
16	LF bk DC agst LOD	Q
	Cross RF in front of LF	Q
	LF bk DC agst LOD	Q
	Close RF to LF	Q
	(Lady: RF fwd DC agst LOD; cross LF	
	behind RF; RF fwd DC agst LOD comm	
	to turn R; LF closes to RF swivelling	
	on RF to R to starting position)	

11,12 *Sways to L and R, chassés to shadow hold*

In bar 11 the partners sway in double hold to man's L (down LOD) then to man's R.

In bar 12 the man moves his LF to the side, closes RF to LF and releases double hold. He then repeats these two steps taking up shadow hold (partners side-by-side, L hands joined with man's RH on lady's waist).

13,14 *Diagonal runs to R and L*

Both man and lady take 4 quick steps diagonally to wall pivoting ½ turn to L on the last step (bar 13). Bar 14 is a repeat of bar 13 moving this time to the centre and pivoting ½ turn R.

A common variation is to tap the foot at the end of bars 13 and 14.

15,16 *Walk, check, back lock*

In bar 15 the man moves LF fwd releasing hold (the lady turns L); then checks outside the lady on her R side with his RF, in double hold again.

In bar 16 he recovers his weight to his LF and takes a back lock step (RF crossing in front of his LF). The sequence ends with man LF bk, close RF to LF.

Summary of the Balmoral Blues

Chassé and zig-zag in double hold. Forward lock down LOD. Outward turn to forward lock. Repeat figures against LOD. Change of place and return (lady allemandes to L and to R). Sways to L and R in double hold. Two chassés taking up shadow hold. Diagonal runs to wall and centre with pivots. Walk and check taking up double hold. Back lock.

GEORGELLA BLUES

DANCE SCRIPT
BARS 1-8

Arranged by Stella and George Berwick in 1950

Ballroom hold, man facing, lady backing LOD. Man's steps described. This dance (and the Bossa Nova Blues which follows) are danced at the faster tempo of 40-42 bpm - almost quickstep speed.

Bar		Count
1-4	**Walks and Half Squares**	
1	LF fwd; RF fwd down LOD	SS
2	LF to side to C; close RF to LF	QQ
	LF fwd	S
3	RF fwd; LF fwd	SS
4	RF to side to wall; close LF to RF	QQ
	RF fwd down LOD turning slightly to R to face DW preparing to step outside partner on L side (loose hold)	S
5-8	**Lock Step Movement to Promenade Position**	
5	LF fwd DW on lady's L side, check	S
	RF bk DC agst LOD	S
6	LF bk; cross RF in front of LF	QQ
	LF bk	S
7	RF bk DC agst LOD and check	S
	LF fwd DW (lady still on man's L side)	S
8	RF fwd DW; cross LF behind RF	QQ
	RF fwd across body turning lady into PP	S
9-12	**Promenade Points - Solo Telemark Turn**	
9	LF fwd down LOD in PP; point RF fwd	SS
10	RF fwd; point LF fwd	SS
11	LF fwd down LOD turning to L releasing hold and facing C	S
	RF to side down LOD still turning L facing DC agst LOD	S
12	LF bk down LOD fcg agst LOD taking lady's R hand in L hand	S
	Point RF fwd agst LOD (body fcg DW agst LOD)	S

Bar   Count

13-16 Solo Telemark Turn - Rotary Chassés
13   RF fwd against LOD turning to R and   S
      releasing hold, body fcg C
      LF to side still tng R, fcg DC   S
14   RF bk agst LOD almost fcg DW   S
      Point LF fwd down LOD taking up   S
      ballroom hold in PP
15   LF to side across LOD turning R,   Q
      partner square
      Close RF to LF   Q
      LF bk still turning   S
16   RF to side and fwd facing DC   Q
      Close LF to RF   Q
      RF fwd down LOD   S

In some areas the half squares of bars 2 and 4 are
replaced by lock steps or chassés.

Another modification is to release hold and clap twice at
the end of bar 12.

Summary of the Georgella Blues

1,2   Forward walks, half square (or lock step or
      chassé).
3,4   Repeat on opposite feet moving to lady's L side.

5,6   LF fwd, check back, back lock.
7,8   RF fwd, check forward, forward lock.

9,10 Steps and points in PP.
11,12 Slow solo turn L (lady turns R). Point RF.
      (Clap twice.)

13,14 Slow solo turn R (lady turns L). Point LF.
      (Bars 11 and 12 repeated on opposite feet.)
15,16 Natural rotary chassé turn.

Betty Croasdale and Fred Dawson (1972)

Loose ballroom hold. Man facing W, lady facing C.
Man's steps described. Time 4/4. Tempo 40 bpm.

Bar   Count

1-4   Clockwise Squares finishing in PP
1   LF fwd; side RF; close LF to RF   SQQ
2   RF bk; side LF; close RF to LF   SQQ
3,4 Bars 1 and 2 repeated finishing in PP

5-8   Man's Open Locks - Lady's Quarter Turn
Closes
5   LF down LOD, lady's RH held high by   QQS
     man's LH; lock RF bhd LF; LF fwd (ss)
6   RF fwd along LOD; lock LF behind RF;   QQS
     RF fwd swaying L and R, L and R
     (Lady: Bar 5: RF fwd turning to face W;
     side LF along LOD; close RF to LF   SQQ
     Bar 6: LF fwd tng to face C and partner;
     side RF along LOD; close LF to RF   SQQ)
7,8 Man and lady repeat steps of bars 5,6

9-16 Promenade Walks - Chicken Walks with
Turning Hips - Clockwise Square - Check and
Close
9   LF fwd along LOD; RF fwd   SS
10   LF fwd with slight body turn inwards;   QQS
     cross RF over LF; side LF along LOD
11,12 Repeat bars 9 and 10 starting on RF
     and finishing facing wall and partner
13,14 Repeat bars 1 and 2 opening out to PP
     facing LOD
15   LF fwd DC (lady DW); RF across LF   SS
     with checking action
16   Replace wt to LF in CBMP turning to   SQQ
     face DW; side RF towards wall and
     partner; close LF to RF without weight

CHAPTER 11

LATIN-AMERICAN DANCES

Latin-America comprises those parts of South and Central America, Mexico and the Caribbean Islands which have Spanish or Portuguese as their official language. The Latin-American dances from these areas have a strong compulsive rhythm and are readily adapted to sequence form. The most important styles for the aspiring sequence dancer to study are the rumba, cha cha cha and jive. Among the 270 new official dances from 1990 to 1995 there were 39 rumbas, 28 cha cha chas, 15 jives, 6 sambas and 2 bossa novas.

The rumba (or rhumba) is a very old dance with African and Cuban origins. There are two main ballroom forms - the American or square rumba (1931) and the Cuban rumba (1948); the latter is the version used by modern ballroom and sequence dancers. The rumba became popular in the United States and Britain in the 1930's. It is danced with a smooth supple hip movement with small heavy walking steps. Sequence rumbas are played at 26-32 bpm. The Variety Rumba (1949) is a very early sequence rumba.

The cha cha cha, sometimes called the Cuban mambo, is a type of rumba with the slow step replaced by a chassé. Its name derives from the basic rhythm of step, step, chassé - often expressed as 'step, step, cha cha cha'. It appeared in America in the 1950's and in Britain in the early 1960's. It is a staccato lively dance giving much room for personal expression. Early sequence forms are the Jacqueline Cha Cha (1961) and the Margarite Cha Cha (1962). The Sally Ann Cha Cha (1973) is popular in the clubs; it has been adopted as a championship dance.

RUMBA ROYALE (ROYAL)

The original music for this dance was the 'Carioca Rumba' and the flick movements are called carioca steps in some scripts. (The carioca is a Brazilian dance something like the samba.) The music has 4 beats per bar and the timing used in the scripts is Q=1 beat, S=2 beats.

RUMBA ROYALE　　　　DANCE SCRIPT BARS 1-6
Nancy Clarke (1964)

Start in loose ballroom hold. Man facing, lady backing down LOD. Man's steps described, lady counterpart unless otherwise stated. Tempo 30-32 bpm.

Bar		Count
1-4	**Clockwise Square - Drag Closes**	
1	LF fwd down LOD	S
	RF to side to wall	Q
	Close LF to RF parallel position	Q
2	RF back against LOD	S
	LF to side towards C	Q
	Close RF to LF, parallel position	Q
3	LF to side towards C	S
	Drag (close) RF to LF ww, releasing hold	S
4	RF to side towards wall, short step	S
	Close LF to RF ww	S
5,6	**Man Moves Down LOD, Lady Against LOD - Partners Pass R Shoulder to R Shoulder**	
5	LF fwd down LOD	Q
	RF fwd down LOD	Q
	LF fwd down LOD, short steps	Q
	Flick RF forward	Q
6	Back RF	Q
	Back LF against LOD	Q
	RF diag back against LOD	Q
	Flick LF to side towards C - now in PP	Q

Bar   Count

7-8   **Partners Move Square to C then to Wall**
7   Fwd LF   Q
         Fwd RF to C   Q
         Fwd LF, tng to R (inwards), releasing RH   Q
         Flick RF towards wall (carioca step)   Q
8   Fwd RF   Q
         LF towards wall   Q
         RF fwd turn L to face down LOD   Q
         Flick LF to C   Q

RUMBA ROYALE   **NOTES ON BARS 1-8**

1-4   *Clockwise square, drag closes*
       A similar start to the Square Tango - a clockwise
       square (bars 1 and 2) followed by a long drag step
       to centre and a RF close without weight (bar 3).
       In bar 4 hold is released and the partners separate
       taking a side step and a close without weight - man
       moves to centre, lady to wall.

5,6   *Forward and backward solo walks, man down
       LOD, lady against LOD*
       In this unusual feature the man walks forward LF,
       RF, LF and flicks his RF fwd. As he does so he
       will see the lady from the couple in front moving
       towards him - often they will touch hands and
       smile. The man checks and repeats the steps
       backwards to rejoin his partner.

7,8   *Partners move square to C, then to wall*
       Man and lady are now in loose ballroom hold in
       promenade position. They move towards the
       centre, the man's steps being LF, RF fwd, LF
       turning R, flick RF to wall. These steps are
       repeated on the opposite foot towards the wall.

Bar   Count

9-16   Allemandes - Natural Rotary Chassé Turns

Bar		Count
9	LF to side twds C, short step	Q
	Move RF twds LF, turn lady to R	Q
	under L hand (lady's R hand)	
	(Lady: RF fwd, tng R; side LF, fcg down	
	LOD; RF back twds C, face wall approx.)	
	Side LF	S
10	RF to side twds wall	Q
	Close LF twds RF, turning partner to L	Q
	under L hand	
	RF fwd ss	S
	(Lady: LF fwd turning L; side RF to face	
	DC down LOD; LF short step to side)	
11	LF to side twds wall, turning R	Q
	Close RF to LF parallel position, back LOD	Q
	LF back down LOD turning to R	S
12	RF to side along LOD to face C	Q
	Close LF to RF parallel position	Q
	RF fwd dn LOD ss, turn partner to PP	S

13-16   Bars 7,8,9,10 repeated ending square to
partner in commencing position

RUMBA ROYALE   NOTES ON BARS 9-12

9,10   *Allemandes*
Sideways steps to centre turning lady to R (man's
LH holding lady's RH).
Sideways steps to wall turning lady to L under
raised LH.

11,12   *Natural rotary chassé turns*
Step, close, step turning ⅜ R repeated as in the
Mayfair Quickstep and Sindy Swing.

Allemande (Alemana)

Lady turning under man's raised hand.

The name 'allemande' comes from an old dance (1549) in which hands were held throughout. It usually now indicates a turn by the lady under the man's raised arm - it involves a change of place. In Latin-American dances it is called the alemana.

In the rumba and cha cha cha the lady usually turns to the R in the alemana. Turns to the L under the man's raised hand are found in the hockey stick (Rumba Rosalie bar 8) and the spiral.

Summary of the Rumba Royale

Loose ballroom hold - clockwise square, drag closes. Solo forward and backward walks. Walks with flicks to centre and wall. Allemandes to centre and wall. Chassé turn. Walk with flicks and allemandes repeated.

RUMBA ROSALIE   DANCE SCRIPT BARS 1-10
Arranged by Eddie Whinfield

Commence in normal hold, man facing, lady backing down LOD. Man's steps described, lady counterpart unless otherwise stated. Time 4/4. Tempo 30-32 bpm.

Bar   Count

1-6   Rumba Walks - Outside Checks
1	LF, RF, LF fwd	2.3.41
2	RF, LF, RF fwd	2.3.41
3	LF fwd DW on partner's L	2
	Replace weight to RF	3
	LF to side turning to face LOD	41
4	RF fwd DC on partner's R	2
	Replace weight to LF	3
	RF to side turning to face LOD	41
5	Repeat bar 3	2.3.41
6	Repeat bar 4 turning to R to face partner and wall on last step	2.3.41

7-12   Side Walk with Lady's Turn - Fwd Rocks
7	LF to side along LOD	2
	Close RF to LF	3
	Side LF releasing man's RH hold	41
8	Repeat bar 7 agst LOD turning lady to L under man's LH	2.3.41
9	LF fwd agst LOD still holding lady's RH in LH	2
	Replace weight back to RF	3
	Replace weight forward to LF turning ½ L to face down LOD and changing hands (rock action)	41
10	RF fwd dn LOD (lady's LH in man's RH)	2
	Replace weight to LF	3
	Replace weight fwd on to RF	41

The timing of all bars in this dance is 2.3.41 (QQS) starting on the 2nd beat of the bar (see page 179).

1,2   *Forward rumba walks*
Bars 1 and 2 are six forward walking steps timed
QQS,QQS. They are short heavy steps taken more
from the legs and feet rather than the gliding steps
of the waltz and slow foxtrot. The ball of the foot
touches the ground first immediately followed by
a full transfer of weight to the full foot - heel leads
are not used in rumbas.

3-6   *Outside checks to L and R (shoulder to shoulder)*
Bars 3 and 4 are checks outside partner to L and R
with a side step in between; these are repeated in
bars 5 and 6 finishing facing wall and partner.
Similar figures are found in many dances such as
the Cathrine Waltz and Caribbean Foxtrot. Outside
checks with a chassé occur in the Mayfair
Quickstep and Sindy Swing (see foot diagram on
page 85).

7,8   *Side walks, side walks with lady's turn to L*
(hockey stick)
Bar 7 is LF to side, close RF to LF, LF to side
moving down LOD.
Bar 8 is the movement repeated starting with the
RF and turning the lady to the L under the raised
L arm (man's LH holds lady's RH) - called a
hockey stick in some scripts.

9,10   *Forward rocks along and against LOD*
Bar 9 is a LF rock against LOD. After a LF fwd
step the man transfers his weight to his RF then
forward to his LF turning L to face down LOD
and changing hands.
Bar 10 is a RF forward rock down LOD.

Bar   Count

11-16 Cucarachas - Forward Basic - Natural Top - Rope Spinning

11	Side LF to C (relax R knee)	2
	Replace weight to RF turning ½ R to face agst LOD changing hands	3
	Close LF to RF	4 1
12	Side RF to C (relax L knee)	2
	Replace weight to LF turning ½ L	3
	Close RF to LF fcg W and partner and taking up rumba hold	4 1
13	LF fwd to W	2
	Replace weight to RF	3
	LF to side and sltly fwd turning R to face DW agst LOD (Lady: RF fwd between partner's feet)	4 1
14	Place RF to heel of LF	2
	Side LF turning R	3
	Close RF to LF now facing LOD (lady walks round on man's R side - LF, RF, LF)	4 1
15	Raise L arm and release hold with R hand, step LF fwd down LOD	2
	Replace weight to RF	3
	LF to side and slightly back (lady walks round RF, LF, RF behind man)	4 1
16	RF back agst LOD	2
	Replace weight to LF to side	3
	Close RF to LF regaining rumba hold (lady walks round LF, RF, LF curving R to end facing partner taking starting hold and position)	4 1

11,12 *Cucarachas to centre*

The cucaracha (beetle crusher) is a pressure step with part weight often taken to the side. Bar 11 is this figure taken LF to centre followed by a ½ turn to the R. Bar 12 is a side RF cucaracha to centre turning to take up rumba hold.

13,14 *Forward basic, natural top*

Bar 13 is a forward basic consisting of LF fwd, weight replaced to RF, LF to side - it is a type of checked forward walk. It is a neat compact step - the replace step is a raising and lowering of the heel without travel. The forward basic is often followed by a natural top in which the man starts to turn R crossing his RF behind his LF. The lady walks round him on his L side unwinding the man as he takes a step to side and closes (something like a twist turn).

15,16 *Basics, rope spinning*

The man takes a forward and a back basic with his L arm raised and held by the lady's RH as she walks round him. The figure is like a man spinning a lasso round his body; it finishes in rumba hold facing down LOD.

Summary of the Rumba Rosalie

Rumba walks (2 bars). Outside checks to L and R repeated (4 bars). Side steps, side steps with lady's turn. Rocks down and agst LOD. LF side cucaracha and R turn, RF side cucaracha. Forward basic, natural top. Forward and back basic - lady walks round man under raised arms (rope spinning).

The Rumba Rosalie dances well to jive music.

RUMBA ONE   DANCE SCRIPT BARS 1-8
Arranged by Peter Varley (1971)

Rumba hold with man facing wall. Man's steps described.
Time 4/4. Tempo 28 bpm.

Bar		Count
1-4	**Forward Basic - Alemana - Shoulder to Shoulder**	
1	LF fwd leaving RF in place	2
	Replace weight back to RF	3
	LF to side raising L arm	4 1
2	RF bk to C allowing lady to turn R under raised LH (alemana)	2
	Replace weight fwd to LF to W	3
	RF to side tng ⅛ to R, partner now square, take up rumba hold fcg DW agst LOD	4 1
3	LF fwd OP on L side, check	2
	Replace weight to RF, comm to turn L	3
	LF to side and slightly fwd fcg DW	4 1
4	RF fwd OP on R side, check	2
	Replace weight to LF, comm to turn R	3
	RF to side, slightly fwd fcg DW agst LOD	4 1
5-8	**Shoulder to Shoulder ending in PP Fencing Line - Solo Turn - Back Walks**	
5	LF fwd OP on L side, check	2
	Replace weight to RF, comm to turn L	3
	LF to side and slightly fwd in PP fcg DW	4 1
6	RF fwd and across in PP (joined rear hands extended backwards to give fencing line)	2
	Replace weight to LF, comm to turn R	3
	RF to side fcg lady and W with man's LH holding lady's RH	4 1
7	LF fwd turning strongly to R releasing hold and leading lady to turn L	2
	RF fwd still turning R	3
	LF fwd to face W and partner, join RHs	4 1
8	RF bk comm to curve to back LOD	2
	LF bk still turning	3
	RF bk backing LOD (¼ turn L over 3 steps)	4 1

This is a rumba in the modern style - it has rumba figures and there is less repetition than in the Rumba Rosalie. The timing for each bar is 2.3.41, that is QQS where Q=1 beat, S=2 beats.

1,2   *Forward basic, alemana*
       Bar 1 is a forward basic for the man and a back basic for the lady.
       In bar 2 the man releases his R hand hold and does a back basic turning the lady to the R under his raised L hand - this is the alemana (see page 169). Many rumbas start with these two figures.

3-6   *Shoulder to shoulder, fencing line*
       In bars 3 and 4 the man checks to L and R of the lady maintaining rumba hold.
       This is repeated in bars 5 and 6 but the final bar has a fencing-line finish - this is an inside check in PP with the rearward hands extended.
       In the **shoulder to shoulder** the man checks outside the lady on either side with a step or chassé in between (see page 85).
       The **New York** is similar in some respects but both man and lady check forward and backward at the same time. Both turn outward as they check (see page 185).

7,8   *Outward solo turns, back walks*
       Releasing hold man and lady turn outwards (man turns R, lady to L); the man finishes facing the wall and partner. They join right hands in handshake hold.
       In bar 8 the man takes 3 curving walks backward making a ¼ turn to L to finish backing LOD while the lady does the corresponding steps forward.

Bar   Count

9-12 Rock - Progressive Walks Forward
        - Side Cucarachas

9   Replace weight fwd to LF   2
      Replace weight bk to RF   3
      Replace weight fwd to LF   4 1
10   RF fwd fcg agst LOD, comm turn L   2
      LF fwd still turning   3
      RF fwd, fcg wall, completing ¼ to L   4 1
      over last 3 steps
11   LF to side with part weight   2
      (strong hip movement)
      Replace weight to RF   3
      LF closes to RF   4 1
12   RF to side with part weight   2
      (strong hip movement)
      Replace weight to LF   3
      RF closes to LF   4 1

13-16 Side Step to Progressive Walks in
        Shadow Position - Solo Turn

13   LF to side   2
      RF closes to LF   3
      LF to side and sltly fwd turning ¼ to L   4 1
      to face LOD, releasing hold with RH and
      turning lady to R - man places his RH on
      lady's R shoulder blade and holds her LH
      in his LH (Lady: RF fwd turning ¼ to R
      to face LOD extending her R arm to side)
14   RF fwd, facing LOD; LF fwd   2.3
      RF fwd   4 1
15   LF fwd; RF fwd   2.3
      LF fwd comm turn L, leading lady to   4 1
      turn to her R, releasing hold
16   RF fwd turning to L   2
      LF fwd still turning   3
      RF fwd turning to face partner and wall,   4 1
      taking normal hold

9,10   *Rock, progressive walks forward*
        Bar 8 ends with RF bk backing LOD.
        Bar 9 is a rock forward on to LF, back to RF and
        forward again on to LF.
        Bar 10 is 3 forward curving walks RF, LF, RF
        turning ¼ L to finish facing wall.

        Variation (bars 8-10) - Many dancers take the
        backwards steps of bar 8 to centre and rock
        forward towards the wall on bar 9, moving
        forwards to the wall on bar 10. Cutting out the
        curves and turns (as in the Broadway Quickstep)
        tends to lead to less confusion on a crowded floor.

11,12   *Side cucarachas*
        These are pressure steps to L and R with transfer
        of weight but no foot travel.

13-16   *Side step, progressive walks in shadow position,
        outward solo turns*
        Bar 13 is LF to side, RF closes to LF, LF to side
        turning the lady into shadow position facing down
        LOD. (Side-by-side, LHs joined, man's RH just
        below lady's R shoulder.)
        Bars 14 and 15 consist of 6 forward rumba walks
        timed QQS.QQS.
        Two forward solo turns (man to L, lady to R)
        finishing in closed facing position (bar 16)
        complete the dance.

Summary of the Rumba One

Loose ballroom hold - Forward basic, alemana. Checks to
R, L and R. Fencing line. Outward solo turns. Back walks.
Rock. Forward walks. Cucarachas to R and L. Six rumba
walks in shadow hold. Outward solo turns.

OTHER RUMBAS

Rumba Aquarius (1970)
Ken Park, NCDTA

Open facing position, R hands joined in handshake hold. Man facing, lady backing LOD. Tempo 30/32 bpm.

1-4   Turkish Towel.
5-8   Curving walks to R. Lady's alemana. Shoulder to shoulder.
9-12   Outside swivel. Progressive walks. Solo turn.
13-16 Hand to hand. Hand to hand. Hip twist.

Rumba Beguine (1984)
Annette Sheridan and Ray Reeves, Minehead

Shadow hold facing LOD. Bars 1-8 lady dances same foot as man, then counterpart. Tempo 29 bpm.

1-4   Forward walks. Left and right checks.
5-8   Spot turns ending forward in open position, man's LH holds lady's RH.
9-12   New York. Swivel walks. Solo turn. Fencing line.
13-16 1-3 basic. 7-9 natural top. Natural opening out movement. 4-6 alemana turn overturned to shadow hold.

Rosemount Rumba (1991)
Philip Ainsley and Lorraine Heron, Blackpool

Open facing position with man facing, lady backing wall. Lady counterpart. Tempo 28-31 bpm.

1-4   Basic to change of place. Cucaracha. Progressive walks. Travelling solo turn.
5-8   Change of place. Fencing line. Underarm turns to left and right.
9-12   Fallaway. Swivel walks. Travelling solo turn. Aida.
13-16 Cuban rock. Inward spot turn (overturned). Shoulder to shoulder.

Holds in Latin-American Dances

Walter Laird lists 23 basic positions for starting or ending the dancing figures. There may be:-

No hand hold - solo turns, some Cuban breaks and changes of place.

One hand hold - opposite hands (LH-RH) or same hands, e.g. RH-RH (handshake hold).

Double hand hold - opposite hands (LH-RH) as in parallel facing position or in cuddle hold; same hands as in skating hold or some forms of shadow hold (LH-LH, RH-RH).

Timing

Competition dancers and those who studied in dancing academies start the rumba and the cha cha cha on the second beat - thus the bars in the rumba are counted 2.3.41 (QQS). Most sequence dancers, however, start their Latin-American dances on the first beat with a timing of 1.2.34 as with the modern dances. Using the two methods on the same floor would lead to dances being out of step - one therefore needs to go along with the majority to avoid confusion.

Rumba and Cha Cha Cha Compared

Although very different in character the rumba and cha cha cha share many of the same figures. They are both danced to music with 4 beats per bar but the slow step in the rumba becomes a chassé in the cha cha cha. The beat values per bar are:-

Rumba	1	1	2		
Cha Cha Cha	1	1	½ ½ 1	(chassé)	

The rumba is a single beat and the cha cha cha a triple beat mambo.

Ken and Barbara Street, 1st ISTD, 1973

Start in loose ballroom hold, man facing wall. Man's steps described, lady counterpart unless otherwise stated. Tempo 32 bpm.

Timing - All bars are counted 2.3.4&1 except the lock steps in bar 4 (2&3.4&1) and the zig-zag of bar 13 (2.3.4.1).

Bar

1-5   Forward Basic - Alemana - Hand to Hand - 3 Forward Chassés (or Lock Steps) - Spot Turns

1   LF fwd to wall - check
        Replace wt back to RF
        Chassé LRL along LOD releasing LH hold

2   RF bk raising L arm to turn lady to her R under raised front arms
        Replace wt fwd to LF (lady still turning R)
        Side RF to chassé RLR agst LOD releasing hold and taking lady's LH in RH

3   LF bk agst LOD turning ¼ L on ball of RF (lady turns ¼ R) - side-by-side position
        Replace wt to RF (check in fallaway position)
        LF fwd to chassé LRL down LOD

4   RF fwd to chassé RLR   (2&3)
        LF fwd to chassé LRL   (4&1)

(The last 3 forward chassés may be taken as lock steps with man turning ⅛ to L, R and L alternately (lady turns in opposite directions)

5   RF fwd releasing hold and starting to turn L (lady turns R)
        Keeping LF in place turn ½ to L replacing wt to LF
        RF to side to chassé RLR still turning L to finish facing lady and DW agst LOD

1,2   *Forward basic, alemana, inward solo spot turns*
The forward basic of bar 1 is LF fwd, weight replaced to RF followed by a chassé LRL (small steps). It is the rumba basic step with the last slow step being replaced by the cha cha chassé.

In bar 2 the man does a back basic turning the lady to the R under raised hands (man's LH holding lady's RH).

Many sequence cha chas start with a forward basic and lady's alemana.

3   *1,2 hand to hand, forward chassé*
The first 2 steps of bar 3 are the beginning of a backward checked movement into fallaway called the hand to hand. (In the full movement this is followed by a chassé (cha cha) or side step (rumba) followed by the corresponding steps in the opposite direction with a change of hands.) The last 3 steps are a cha cha chassé LRL down LOD often taken with a locking action and a body turn first to R then to L with appropriate hand and arm movements.

4   *Two forward chassés*
Two more forward cha cha chassés RLR and LRL consisting of 6 steps timed '2&3.4&1'.

5   *Chassé solo turns*
The man turns outward to the L, the lady outward to the R. Solo turns in Latin-American dances are turning basics without hand hold. (There are 3 turning walks in the rumba and 2 turning walks and a chassé in the cha cha cha.) They may be spot turns as in this case or involve travel down or against the LOD.

Bar

6-10   Follow My Leader

6   LF fwd fcg DW agst LOD taking lady's RH in LH
Replace wt to RF
LF bk to chassé LRL backing DC

7   RF bk releasing hold (lady turns R)
Replace wt to LF
RF fwd to chassé RLR facing DW agst LOD
(Lady: LF fwd turning ½ R to face DW agst LOD
ending with back to man; replace wt to RF; LF
fwd to chassé LRL facing DW agst LOD)

8   LF fwd facing DW agst LOD turning ½ R to face
DC (lady turns L)
Replace wt to RF
LF fwd to chassé LRL facing DC
(Lady: RF fwd turning ½ L to face DC; replace wt
to LF; RF fwd to chassé RLR facing DC - now
behind man)

9   RF fwd turning ½ L to face DW agst LOD (lady
turns R)
Replace wt to LF
RF fwd to chassé RLR facing DW agst LOD
(Lady: LF fwd turning ½ R to face DW agst LOD
ending with back to man; replace wt to RF; LF
fwd to chassé LRL facing DW agst LOD)

10   LF fwd facing DW agst LOD (lady turns L)
Replace wt to RF
LF to side to chassé LRL turning ⅛ L to face W
and taking lady's LH in RH
(Lady: RF fwd turning ½ L to face DC now facing
man; replace wt to LF turning slightly L; RF to
side to chassé RLR to face C)

6-9 *Follow my leader*

In bar 6 the man checks and chassés LRL moving backwards towards DC (the lady chassés forward RLR). The scripts state that man's LH should hold lady's RH but this hold is sometimes omitted.

Bars 7, 8, 9 are the essential 'follow my leader' movement. The partners follow one behind the other in tandem position moving forward in a straight line. Each bar starts with a step and replace (a check) sometimes with a ½ turn by one or both partners; this is followed by the three steps of a cha cha cha forward chassé. Both turn opposite ways.

In bar 7 the lady turns ½ R and chassés forward LRL moving DW agst LOD. The man follows behind the lady and chassés RLR.

In bar 8 both partners make a half turn - man to R, lady to L - and chassé back again towards DC with man in front and lady behind.

In bar 9 the man turns ½ L, the lady ½ R and they chassé back again towards DW agst LOD. On the first step the more boisterous men may stamp their foot, raise their right hand and shout "Oi!".

10 *Check and chassé turning to open hold*

The man checks and chassés LRL to face the wall taking the lady's LH in his RH in open hold. The lady turns left and chassés RLR to finish facing centre.

Bar

11-16 New York - Zig-Zag - Cross Basics with Change of Place - Spot Turns

11   RF fwd turning ¼ to L to face LOD (check)
Replace wt to LF turning R (lady turns L)
RF to side agst LOD to chassé RLR to finish facing W, changing hands to take lady's RH in LH (lady turns ¼ L to face C)

12   LF fwd turning ¼ to R to face agst LOD (check) - side-by-side position
Replace wt to RF turning L (lady turns R)
LF to side along LOD to chassé LRL to finish facing W taking up double hold (lady turns ¼ R to face C)

13   RF fwd and across in PP moving down LOD
LF to side turning ¼ R to back DC
RF bk behind LF turning L (lady turns R)
LF to side completing L turn to face down LOD releasing hold

14   RF fwd turning ¼ L to face C
Replace wt to LF turning R
RF to side to chassé RLR passing behind lady to finish with RF to side facing DW

15   LF turning R to face W
Replace wt to RF turning L
LF to side to chassé LRL passing behind lady to finish with LF to side facing down LOD

16   RF fwd down LOD turning L (lady turns R)
Keeping LF in place turn ½ to L replacing weight to LF to face agst LOD
Chassé RLR to finish facing lady and wall

11,12 *New York*

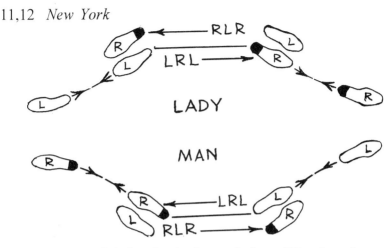

Man and lady check forward from PP, chassé to the side changing inside hands and check on the opposite side.

13   *Zig-zag (or weave).*
        The man turns to R and then to L in four steps timed 2.3.4.1 (1 beat per step).

14-16 *Cross basics (changes of place), spot turns*
       In bar 14 the man chassés sideways to the wall passing behind the lady (no hold) and checks; the lady does the corresponding steps moving to the C. The procedure is reversed in bar 15 - see man's steps in the diagram above.
       Bar 16 is the outward solo turn of bar 5.

Summary of the Sally Ann Cha Cha

Forward and back basics (Lady: alemana). Check back in fallaway. Three forward chassés. Outward spot turns. Follow my leader. New York. Zig-zag. Changes of place. Outward spot turns.

OTHER CHA CHA CHAS

WHEELS CHA CHA (1961)

Music 'Wheels Cha Cha', Norman Petty/Joe Loss

Start in double hold with man facing down LOD.

Bar

1   LF, RF fwd; chassé LRL fwd
2   RF, LF fwd; chassé RLR turning to face wall in counter promenade position on last step
3   LF fwd to wall; replace wt to RF releasing hold and turning L; chassé LRL still turning
4   Side RF to centre (small step) turning L; LF fwd to wall still turning; chassé RLR to side to W taking up double hold
5   Turning to face centre, whisk LF behind RF; RF fwd turning inwards to face LOD and partner; chassé LRL sideways to centre
6   Turning to face wall repeat bar 5 on opposite feet finishing by a sideways chassé RLR to wall
7,8   Release lady's LH and dance on the spot while lady moves round clockwise making almost a full turn - adopt the original hold

This dance is often used for teaching the cha cha cha to beginners; it can also be performed as a rumba by replacing the chassés by single steps.

COMMADOR CHA CHA (1992)
Michael and Ann Morris, ADA

Closed facing position with man fcg wall. Tempo 32 bpm.

Bar
1-4   Forward basic. Alemana. Side rock. Zig-zag.
5-8   Spot turn. Check to change of place. Forward basic. Spot turn to counter shadow hold.
9-12   Back basic. Back basic (lady change of place). Fencing line. Flick tap. Swivel cross.
13-16   Cha cha locking chassés. Solo turn. Basic to natural top.

THE JIVE

'Jive' is a general term covering several related dances played to various rhythms in the tempo range 20-60 bpm. The modern sequence jive has its own figures and ballroom technique. It is danced to music in 4/4 time within the tempo range of 35-46 bpm. It is really a North-American rather than a Latin-American dance but it resembles the rumba and cha cha cha in some respects and is conveniently placed in the same class. It has a triple beat rhythm like the cha cha cha (the rock and roll is a single beat form like the rumba).

The Rock Barn Dance and the Rumba Rosalie can be used to give practice in the jive.

ROCK BARN DANCE   **DANCE SCRIPT**
                                       BARS 1-16

Open hold with hands joined, man facing wall, lady facing centre. Tempo 35-46 bpm.

Bar		Count
1	Chassé LRL along LOD	QQS
2	Chassé RLR agst LOD	QQS
3	Chassé along LOD turning lady under man's L arm to L (alemana)	QQS
4	Chassé agst LOD turning lady under man's L arm to R (alemana)	QQS
5	LF to side along LOD	S
	Swing RF across LF and clap	S
6	RF to side agst LOD	S
	Swing LF across RF and clap	S
7,8	Repeat bars 5 and 6 turning into PP	SS SS
9,10	Take 6 jive walks along LOD	SQQ SQQ
11,12	Repeat bars 9 and 10	SQQ SQQ
13,14	Walk 3 slow steps to centre LRL and clap (Lady: walks 3 steps to wall and claps)	SS SS
15,16	Walk 3 slow steps twds partner RLR and clap taking up starting hold	SS SS

Section III

THE LIGHTER SIDE OF SEQUENCE DANCING

by TITANIUS

'Titanius' is a contributor of articles to 'The Ballroom Dancing Times'; he is author of a standard work on aeronautics and a composer of humorous verses. In this section he has taken a light-hearted look at some aspects of dancing technique and ballroom etiquette. With its accompanying cartoons it does much to lighten the treatment of what is, to some extent, a serious and demanding pastime.

LES BARTON

Born in 1923, Les Barton's first published cartoon appeared in the *Militant Miner* in 1944; his first *Punch* cartoon followed in 1954.

Over the years, he has been an illustrator of children's comics and annuals, working for both DC Thomson and IPC, and has written and drawn numerous famous comic strips, including *Billy Bunter, Ma Kelly's Telly, Harry's Haunted House* and *I Spy.* His work has also appeared in *Private Eye, The Spectator,* and *The Times Magazine,* and is syndicated around the world.

He spends most of his day at the drawing board, scribbling down thoughts and mulling over ideas for the many greetings cards he designs and produces for *Camden Graphics* and *Cardtoons.* In between, he originates cartoons in his well-known and very distinctive style.

Chapter 12

POISE AND HOLD

Both ballroom and sequence dances are partner dances and for the most part man and lady have some sort of contact. There are several old-time dancing holds and many more used in Latin American dances like the rumba and cha cha cha. Ballroom hold is, however, the most common. An important factor in this is poise - the position of the body in relation to the feet.

In simple ballroom hold the man's body is inclined slightly forward from the feet upwards so the weight is mainly on the balls of the feet. The lady's poise is slightly backward with some weight being felt on the heels - to retain balance she needs some support from the man in this position.

There are many variations in ballroom hold which are of interest (and sometimes mild amusement!) to the observer. Some of these are illustrated as dancing types in the following pages.

DANCING TYPES NO. 1: THE FORWARD LEANER

Probably wants to move faster but is doubtful about the next figure; or perhaps he wants to whisper sweet nothings into his partner's ear?

Highly trained dancers often adopt poises which deviate more from the vertical.

Ballroom Dancing

The 'big-top' line

Early Tango

Argentine Tango

Any marked deviation from a vertical poise will increase body contact - no-one can lean forward or backward without some support from the partner's arms and body. The modern 'English' style attaches great importance to firm body contact. It is not easy to take long steps, turn well and maintain a good body line if there is 'daylight' between the partners. In go-as-you-please dances the man has to lead his partner into the various dancing figures by subtle movements of his arm and body and a close hold is essential. In sequence dancing the roles are more equal - the lady knows the sequence and will often help the man; body contact is less important.

DANCING TYPES NO. 2: THE BATTLEAXE

She does the leading.
Will lift her partner into place if necessary.

Another aspect of close body contact may be good or bad depending on your point of view. Much so-called 'crush dancing' is an excuse for a man to embrace a partner closely in public - dancing takes second place to social interaction. Sequence and old-time dancers adopt the older tradition of maintaining some distance between the partners.

CASTLE HOUSE SUGGESTIONS
FOR CORRECT DANCING

Do not wriggle the shoulders.

Do not shake the hips.

Do not twist the body.

Do not flounce the elbows.

Do not pump the arms.

Do not hop—glide instead.

Avoid low, fantastic, and acrobatic dips.

Stand far enough away from each other to allow free movement of the body in order to dance gracefully and comfortably.

The gentleman should rest his hand lightly against the lady's back, touching her with the finger-tips and wrist only, or, if preferred, with the inside of the wrist and the back of the thumb.

The gentleman's left hand and forearm should be held up in the air parallel with his body, with the hand extended, holding the lady's hand lightly on his palm. The arm should never be straightened out.

Remember you are at a social gathering, and not in a gymnasium.

Drop the Turkey Trot, the Grizzly Bear, the Bunny Hug, etc. These dances are ugly, ungraceful, and out of fashion.

From 'Modern Dancing'
by Mr. and Mrs. Vernon Castle, 1914

DANCING TYPES NO. 3: THE HIGH KICKER

DANCING TYPES NO. 4: THE STAMPER

Probably an ex-RSM or a Post Office employee. He ruins the mood for other dancers by stamping hard on every side-together movement, or whenever he feels like it. Ladies can be stampers too, but this is generally due to a row with their partner.

DANCING TYPES NO. 5: THE HIGH STEPPER

Tends to lift a bent knee at the wrong times,
particularly when she should be doing a point.

DANCING TYPES NO. 6:
THE INEXPERIENCED JIVERS

This actually happened to the author and his wife at a
sequence dance. Having learnt to do a Change of Hands
Behind the Back at ballroom classes they were so busy
looking at other dancers they did not watch each other!

Chapter 13

DRESS AT DANCES

It would be a bold person who attempted to tell people how to dress for their entertainment, and much would depend on the location and type of dance: people in a stockbroker belt might dress differently from those in a farming community or a seaport.

Farming area~

Stockbroker area~

Dance at seaport~

Those who go to discos are generally in a different age bracket from those who go to ballroom and sequence dances and have their own ideas about dress.

Sequence dancers tend to be in a different age bracket from disco dancers ↝

However, few would dispute that the ladies usually have the right idea and that their ensemble is correct for the occasion, i.e. skirts below the knee (after all, in some dances they should, in theory if not in practice, hold their skirt with the right hand) and no trouser suits. Ladies with no dress sense are, fortunately, very rare and the cartoon exaggerates an extremely unusual occasion.

**DANCING TYPES NO. 7:
LADIES LACKING DRESS SENSE**

*Generally rare birds,
but can cause a sensation when spotted.*

The men should assess the type of dance and dress accordingly, remembering that a dance is a social occasion and that dancing is an art form which should give pleasure to both dancer and onlooker. Keys dangling from belts and sloppy pullovers are not really *de rigueur* for any dance.

Normal wear at local dances or sequence dances is casual although some men wear suits and, indeed, these should be worn in a smart hotel.

DANCING TYPES NO. 8: THE DELICATE HOLDER

One can only imagine that the lady has a well-used handkerchief in her right hand.

In many places it is common practice for the jacket to be removed at the start of the dance and in some clubs the tie will quickly follow, especially in summertime if the hall lacks good ventilation. Since jackets are not being worn it is preferable to have long-sleeved shirts, although short-sleeved ones are common in summer. It goes without saying that belts should be worn, not braces.

DANCING TYPES NO. 9:
THE RELUCTANT DANCER

The man gets dragged along to dances unwillingly.
His thoughts are elsewhere.

When the dance is advertised as a Ball, it is usual to wear evening dress. Having said that, the type of Ball must be looked at. In one organised for its members by a sequence club it will be found that almost everyone wears evening dress; men not wearing a black tie will be thin on the ground. Where there is a Ball in which both sequence dancing and ballroom dancing take place it will often be found that standards of dress will differ widely. To make the matter clearer it is best for the tickets to have printed on them **Black Tie Preferred**.

Shoes are the tools of the trade and the novice dancer will quickly discover those that suit him or her best. Ladies should remember that stiletto heels do not improve the surface of dance floors and they should wear shoes with broader-based heels - indeed entry to a dance floor may be refused to ladies who wear them. Patent leather shoes for the men are no longer common and light shoes with or without perforations in the uppers are now widely used, the soles of these shoes being specially designed for dancing.

If shoes are tools, then the floor is the workbench. Unfortunately, the surfaces vary widely from the perfect floor to ones which are too sticky or too slippery. Sticky ones are rare and the fault can often be rectified by the use of French chalk, if this is permitted. The chalk must be applied with great care to obtain an even distribution - otherwise smooth patches will occur which are very hazardous. The slippery ones are all too common in village halls that are used for other purposes and where a zealous cleaner has been generous with the polish. Paradoxically, the use of polish sometimes makes the floor sticky. Anyway, it is wise to take along a wire brush or a wet rag with which to clean the soles of the shoes.

Chapter 14

SEQUENCE DANCING ETIQUETTE

Unwritten rules of etiquette probably apply less to sequence dancers than to ballroom dancers. Members of sequence dance clubs generally know one another well and have their own partners - they form a closely-knit society and it is well to follow their tribal customs.

On entering a sequence club dance hall for the first time, find out where the regulars sit, and do not go there. Make yourself known to whoever is in charge; he or she will tell you where to sit and may also ask your name so that a welcome can be made to you during the announcements made in the interval.

In Britain it is not the custom to cut in on other dancers when ballroom dancing (for which we must be thankful), although this is common in the USA. It would be unthinkable to cut in on people during a sequence dance unless an announcement is made by the organisers to the effect that the dance is to be an 'Excuse Me' dance, in which case the practice of passing out several articles which are then handed to the partner of the person being excused is a good idea.

In a sequence dance there is no time to discuss the finer points of any figure and if your partner does something which in your opinion is incorrect, by the time you have tried to put your thoughts into words you are into a figure two bars further on and your words of wisdom will not make sense; indeed, your abbreviated explanation might, unintentionally, sound rude. So, forget about the errors for the time being and discuss them later if need be.

A more controversial issue is whether to help dancers having problems with a particular sequence by calling out the dancing figures. Some couples appreciate this while others regard it as an intrusion on their privacy - not only are their deficiencies made more obvious to other dancers but the close scrutiny often has an adverse effect on their performance.

THE MAN WHO TOLD AN EXPERIENCED
DANCER SHE HAD MADE A MISTAKE
After H. M. Bateman

At the end of a dance it is customary for the man to escort his partner back to her seat. The man has a choice of offering an arm, holding the lady's hand or just walking beside her.

Good floorcraft is performing the sequence as correctly as possible having due regard for other dancers in the vicinity. If there is plenty of room, by all means take long steps and extend your arms in the rumba. If the floor is crowded or you are following a couple who take short steps, modify your technique accordingly. If you should happen to bump into other dancers apologise and your apology should be accepted with good grace. Better still, apologise even if you do not think it is your own fault.

IF YOU BUMP INTO SOMEONE
APOLOGISE WITH GOOD GRACE
AND YOUR APOLOGY SHOULD BE ACCEPTED

It goes without saying that dancers should not walk on the dance floor when the MCs are demonstrating. They should also not stand with their backs to the MC, talking to others who are sitting down. By so doing they obscure the view of many who need to see the demonstration.

**DO NOT WALK ACROSS THE DANCE FLOOR
DURING A DEMONSTRATION**

It also goes without saying that at the end of a ballroom dance when one or two groups of people might gather together in conversation they should immediately leave the floor when the next dance is announced. It is regrettable that some people show bad manners by remaining there and getting in the way of other dancers.

DO NOT STAY TALKING ON THE DANCE FLOOR AFTER A NEW DANCE HAS BEEN ANNOUNCED

If you leave, or join, the floor in the middle of a dance it is your responsibility to avoid the other dancers - not the other way round!

Many sequence and club dances have a raffle. This enhances the takings and adds a bit of fun to the proceedings at the interval.

RAFFLES ARE A GOOD METHOD OF GETTING RID OF UNWANTED CHRISTMAS PRESENTS

Generally the dancers bring a small present to augment those supplied by the organisers - the value of the present will be assessed by experience.

When attending some club dances on a regular basis it is wise not to buy too many raffle tickets as the winners are greeted with "Every week!". Winning is attributed to good fortune rather than to having purchased a generous supply of tickets!

Chapter 15

DIFFERENT VENUES -
DIFFERENT RECEPTIONS!

Over a Christmas holiday my wife and I went to three different types of dance in a town which we had not visited for many years. These three venues were of interest because of their very contrast.

The first was a local sequence club dance. It was all we expected it to be. My wife and I were received kindly and made to feel at home. People asked where we were from and chatted to us, and we were even given a piece of Christmas cake and a celebration drink. The dances were similar to ones our local clubs would do and we had a very satisfactory evening's entertainment.

MY WIFE AND I WERE RECEIVED KINDLY

The second dance was held in our hotel. Advertised as a sequence dance, nevertheless it had several ballroom dances as well. The MC was excellent as he asked what dances we would like and was able to demonstrate them all - with one exception which we led ourselves.

The third dance we went to was a bit of a disaster: it was held in a dance studio and perhaps our experience of this sort of venue should have warned us what to expect. The limiting factor of a dance studio is that ballroom dancing is taught there! Nothing wrong in that; the staff, however, give the impression that they are reluctant to teach basic sequence dancing, but that they feel they have an obligation to do so. Unfortunately, they stop right there - at the basics. At one studio I suggested they teach the Red Rose Saunter for a change and the teacher got quite excited and told another teacher that there was a new dance out they could do instead of the Saunter Together. He did not appear to know that there are dozens of saunters! If they have a ball, then almost the only sequence dances they put on are the Saunter Together, the Square Tango, Barn Dance Jive, Rumba One, Melody Foxtrot, Mayfair Quickstep and Sweetheart Waltz - none of the more recent ones.

Anyway, to return to the dance studio which had advertised mixed dancing. Firstly the entrance fee cost three or four times more than that asked at a comparable club or local hall. This I do not complain about for they are trying to make a living and we do not object to paying for good entertainment. There were strict rules, however, which we had not encountered before. Perhaps it is a good idea to change shoes outside in the lobby, at least the stiletto shoes some ladies misguidedly take to dances would not be able to cause damage. Perhaps it is a good idea (can't think why!) not to allow plastic bags to be put under seats. We were not the only sinners in this respect; we were however the only ones to be singled out for correction! We were also asked rather pointedly if we had paid? The normal drill in at least half the clubs we visit is to take the money in the interval; since no-one had been around to pay when we entered this one we replied in the negative. After these one or two sour notes we started to dance.

Now, the trouble with a ballroom dance on a crowded floor is that other people get in the way! If one is doing a particular figure then fate decrees that someone else is bound to be occupying the space one needs to complete it, so the steps have to be changed at the last moment. We coped all right at this place using our highly skilled avoiding actions, always remembering to apologise for a minor bump even if it were not our fault (if only everyone else would do this).

DANCING TYPES NO. 10: THE BATTLESHIP

A large man who ploughs his way through other dancers. He never bumps into them for they see him coming. A rare type nowadays thanks to navy cuts.

Unfortunately, two semi-professionals present seemed determined to take long steps and show their expertise - their dominating presence intimidated the rest of us so that everyone quickly yielded an area equal to a quarter of the total floor space for them to dance in by themselves! During sequence dances, however, we felt a bit smug and superior when these two could not cope with a simple Rumba One; indeed they kept getting in *our* way!

**THE DOMINATING PRESENCE
OF TWO SEMI-PROFESSIONALS
INTIMIDATED THE REST OF US**

Prior to this the sequence dance had been the Mayfair Quickstep and, to our disappointment, the next one to be put on was the Square Tango. We realised that, although our ballroom talents were inferior to those of some of the other dancers, our sequence dancing skills and experience were definitely superior, so we decided to call it a day and go home.

Chapter 16

DANCING IN BENIDORM

Benidorm! Any dancer who has read about the delights of this town in the Costa Blanca could not have failed to notice that Ballroom Dancing and Sequence Dancing are mentioned as two of the attractions. In need of a bit of sun after the wet winter we have experienced lately, my wife and I chose this venue so as to combine our dancing interests with excursions and possibly a glimpse of El Sol. In the case of the latter we were not disappointed; of the dancing we had mixed experiences.

Before I go into details the reader should be aware that most of the big hotels put on dances - either tea dances or sequence and ballroom dances (or both at the same time as we shall see later). *These are free.* An important thing to note is that *all the floors are of marble.* It is, therefore, wise to consider what sort of shoes one should wear for these occasions. With some exceptions, and depending on the amount of space allotted to dancers, the floors have pillars in the middle. Unfortunately, the hotel dances usually take place in what is normally a lounge, or part of one, and open to all the residents, so one must share space with them. They can be seen drinking, playing cards, reading, sitting, or sitting and thinking. Some appear to be taking a keen interest in the dancing; others look mystified. One feature about Benidorm is that the MCs are all up-to-date with the latest sequence dances and will even give teaching sessions. All the hotels are within walking distance - Benidorm is not all that large and a twenty-minute walk is about the maximum one would have to do.

The opinions expressed about the venues are my own. Since other people might have views that do not correspond to mine through going at different times, having different dancing interests or having different MCs I am not naming the hotels concerned. If you can find that rare thing, a rainy afternoon in Benidorm, you could while away an hour or two trying to identify them!

A SEA OF SMOKE HIT US AS WE DESCENDED THE STAIRS ...

In one or two cases we found that our initial impressions were altered after a second or third visit. For example, fairly late in the evening and after being at a dance in another hotel we popped into Hotel A just to see what the situation was there. I got no further than the bottom of the stairs for a sea of smoke was floating around the place and, since I am one of those people who think smoking should be carried out only by consenting adults in private, I backed hurriedly away. On the second visit a day or two later, the amount of smoke was less and, in the interests of readers, we sacrificed some of our life expectancy and sat down. Someone was playing records in the corner of the dance floor. It was possible to dance to some of the tunes he played although the tempi were not always ideal for our type of dancing. In fairness, however, it must be said that his programme seemed to please the dozen or so people there who took to the floor. I asked for a waltz and he did oblige, but put on only one instead of the normal two. Well, all this was not too bad so we went there on another occasion when a sequence dance had been announced. Things were considerably better, the MC had full control and the unusual feature was that sequence dancing took place in the main ballroom area and ballroom dancing took place in an adjacent room using the same music. So if you did not know a particular sequence dance you could still enjoy yourself. The only fly in the ointment was that the sequence dancing area was very crowded - it was so bad that on one or two occasions we had to leave the floor. There were no pillars, which was a blessing, although by getting rid of the people who were only there to watch, the floor could have been made larger but would then have had to include some pillars.

Hotel B uses part of the exit from the restaurant as the dance floor so we had to wait for the diners to leave. The floor is rather narrow so I was surprised when the first dance announced was the Centenary Waltz which requires plenty of space across the floor. It was played too fast for comfort anyway. There was some trouble with the microphone and as the name of the dance was announced only once it was not always easy to know what was to follow. I think the name should always be announced twice - others will have shared my experience of turning to a neighbour and enquiring, "*Which* dance did he say?" No doubt MCs think their words are bell-like, but on occasions in Benidorm some of the asides the MCs made were completely garbled.

Hotel C has sequence dancing one floor down and no directions as to how to get there but we persevered and found it eventually. Some pillars were in the way, but the floor was larger than that of Hotel B - reasonably satisfactory.

Hotel D - With high hopes we descended to the lounge where the dances were held. A wave of heat hit us as we arrived, deflating some of our enthusiasm. Despite being fairly early we had trouble finding chairs; we eventually settled near a large fire exit door to the outside. Just before the dance started a man came along and locked this door, taking away the key. I suppose it will take a catastrophe before the Spanish authorities realise how irresponsible this is. As in Hotel A, the MC announced that the main floor was for sequence dancing and the lounge adjacent to this was for ballroom dancing. However, everyone dancing in the smaller lounge was doing sequence; anyone naive enough to attempt ballroom dancing would probably never be seen alive again. The MCs did their sequence demonstrations in the smaller room and could not be seen by people in the large one. An exception to this was a demonstration of one of the latest dances which was done in both rooms. The air conditioning here coped with the smoke from the many spectators, but it did not manage to cool the air to a comfortable temperature. My wife suffers from the heat even more than I do so we did not stay to the end.

Perhaps the management keep the temperature up so that they sell more drinks. If it is like this in winter, what can it be like in summer?

Hotel E - It was a tea dance we went to here so the dancing was both sequence and ballroom. There were, however, two pillars in the middle of the floor to complicate matters. Anyone dancing nearer the centre of the room rather than on the outside had to move to the outside to get round the pillars so a bottle-neck effect would take place. A pleasant current of air kept us cool. Not too many dancers, but plenty of spectators. It was good entertainment despite the simplicity of the dances.

THE PILLARS TENDED TO GET IN THE WAY ...

We continued our research by visiting another tea dance at Hotel F. A strong smell of fried fish greeted us as we entered. There were two pillars in the middle of the floor and the dance area itself ran right alongside the bar. The floor was smallish and the place rather full. They were doing the Sandringham Saunter as we entered and this was followed by the Sindy Swing which we found was put on at most of the venues we visited.

THE SMELL OF FRIED FISH GREETED US AS WE ENTERED ...

Hotel G got ten out of ten marks for a tea dance we attended on a Sunday. There were no pillars and the floor was large enough; indeed, it could have been enlarged still further by taking the chairs and tables surrounding the floor further back, although some pillars would have then intruded. Only one or two people were smoking and the few spectators included Spaniards sitting in a corner who appeared interested in what we were doing but, for all I know, might have thought us *loco*. The dancing was both sequence and ballroom.

Benidorm has much to commend it - winter sun, cheap food and drink, excellent beaches and many quality shops. The hotels are magnificent and very welcoming - there are no public toilets and washrooms in the resort, it is expected that everyone will make use of the facilities of the nearest hotel. In the same way the afternoon and evening tea and sequence dances can be attended by all for the price of a drink.

In the winter dancing season it is quite safe to walk about in the evening - there is plenty of music and entertainment and a general atmosphere of good-natured enjoyment.

I cannot end this without referring to the Benidorm Palace, a night club with, it is claimed, the largest stage in the world, where there is dancing for members of the audience on the stage before the show and in the interval. The floor is of wood not marble. The music provided was, on this occasion, not the sort that readers of this manual would hope for. Night clubbers and disco dancers might like it, but only small sections of the music programme were suitable for us. However, if you go, enjoy the show, especially if you like flamenco dancing.

DANCING AXIOMS

1. During a ballroom dance other couples will always be occupying the floor space you need to complete your favourite figure.

2. When you are doing a sequence dance that you are not too sure about, the couples in front and behind you have never done it before.

3. If you are doing a sequence dance that you learnt last week, and a couple behind you are trying to copy you because of your apparent skill, you always make a bad mistake.

4. Whenever you make a mistake you find that your MC is watching you.

5. Your MC is never watching you when you think you have danced a sequence particularly well.

6. The difficult sequence dance just announced and which you were taught recently is the one you intended to run through at home, but forgot.

7. If you have done a sequence dance 500 times before, when you come to lead it your mind goes blank.

8. You were in the bar last week when the MC announced that you should all come in evening dress this week.

9. If the MC suggests that you all come in weird clothes next week you will be the only couple to remember.

10. The raffle prize you have just won is the Christmas present you received from your maiden aunt - which you donated last week.

11. When visiting a sequence club that you have never been to before, you find the dances are completely different from the ones normally put on by your own club.

12. The sequence dance just ended and which you have watched from the side in admiration is a dance that you suddenly realise is one that you know quite well.

13. If you receive two scripts in the mail in the morning and practise the waltz, it will be the tango the MC teaches that evening.

14. When you want to check up on a detail in a figure by watching the MCs, *that* is the moment someone comes along to take your raffle money.

15. When all dancing couples are nicely equidistant from each other someone will try to join the floor right in front of you.

16. The people who bump into you towards the end of the dance are the same couple who did it at the beginning - and they are still implying it is your fault!

17. When the MC says to join him on the floor for this dance you boldly step out only to find you have confused the name of the dance with another one.

18. Despite having no bar, the local hall you are visiting will always have a notice saying:-
PLEASE LEAVE THIS HALL IN A REASONABLE CONDITION.

NOTES